GAMECOCK ENCORE

THE 2011 UNIVERSITY OF SOUTH CAROLINA BASEBALL TEAM'S RUN TO BACK-TO-BACK NCAA CHAMPIONSHIPS

TRAVIS HANEY

foreword by BRADY THOMAS

Charleston London

THE
History
PRESS

Published by The History Press
Charleston, SC 29403
www.historypress.net

Copyright © 2012 by Travis Haney
All rights reserved

Cover design by Natasha Walsh

Cover images by Paul Collins

First published 2012

Manufactured in the United States

ISBN 978.1.60949.599.2

Library of Congress CIP data applied for.

To Mimmie
No one will ever empower and encourage like you.
I am forever thankful.

Contents

Foreword

"If you're messing with me, I'll kill you."

I was smiling, but that was what I told Coach Holbrook and Coach Meyers when they let me know I had been granted a sixth year of eligibility from the NCAA. That news led to my third year as a Gamecock—and my second national championship in those three years.

I was getting ready to run the steps at Carolina Stadium when they stopped me. That was part of my self-imposed training plan while I waited to hear about the extra year. It was a lonely feeling, having to train without my teammates, all on my own. Without the NCAA's approval, this would be all that was left of my baseball career. It was a real disappointment to watch from the concourse as my teammates prepared to defend the school's only major national title. It was a national title that I had been part of, that I had helped win. An occasional "Miss you, man" or "Wish you were out here, Brady" only seemed to make the separation worse. For two seasons, I had battled with those guys. Through frigid February evenings in Columbia to blistering June afternoons in Omaha, we were brothers—brothers with a common goal.

Apprehension and anxiety were all I felt when the coaches called me their way that February afternoon. Coach Holbrook and Coach Meyers weren't messing with me. It felt like a dream when I heard Coach Esposito tell me to meet him on the field before practice for one-on-one skill work. I couldn't believe it!

And that's the way my season started, with a lesson learned. From that day forward, I worked hard not to take for granted how blessed I was to walk on any field, much less TD Ameritrade Park.

After I left Florida State, there was a time when I thought I would never play ball again. But Coach Tanner took a chance on me. Because of that, my childhood dream of playing in Omaha would soon become a reality. Not only was he a great coach, but he also taught us so much more than baseball. Perseverance and hard work were two things Coach Tanner instilled in his players. His drive to win was like no other coach I had ever seen before.

Our team was the most well-rounded, humble group that anyone could ever imagine. To be with them for another season meant so much to me. Not long after I got the sixth year, my teammates elected me as one of three captains. Not only would I become a leader of our team, but I would also share the responsibilities with two of my longtime teammates, Scott Wingo and Michael Roth. To be one of the captains with such a close-knit group of guys was an honor.

From 2010 to 2011, the bond between us only got stronger. We expected to win, and we were coached to win every game. "Battle" and "win anyway" did not only become our slogans, they became who we were. We taught each other, as teammates, to be selfless and represent what it means to be a national champion. We certainly weren't the biggest or strongest boys to wear the garnet and black, but I'll guarantee we were the toughest. We never feared any team that opposed us. No one was standing in our way.

There is a passage in Ecclesiastes that speaks of a strand of string that alone is not very strong and easily broken. But when combined with other strings, it becomes a rope that is unbreakable. Each one of us—coaches, trainers, managers and players—was a string. Individually, we were nothing. But put us together?

We were the South Carolina Gamecocks, unbreakable and unbeatable.

Brady Thomas
South Carolina catcher, 2009–11
South Carolina captain, 2011

Author's Note

Iwasn't sure whether I should write this book, even as of November 2011. Please do not misunderstand. I wanted to write it, but life changed pretty dramatically for me about a month after my second time covering the College World Series. I was asked in August to move to Oklahoma to cover Sooners football, a terrific opportunity in my profession at the "tender" age of thirty.

So, as I moved to suburban Oklahoma City, I went back and forth on whether I should write the sequel to *Gamecock Glory*. It had been another incredible run in 2011 for the Gamecocks; there was no doubting that. But would I have time? Would it be too much, considering the move and the Sooners football season?

Ultimately, and obviously, I decided that I should write it. Two reasons: the team's story was again that good, with dramatic victories and personalities that I would never get tired of describing. Whether we're supposed to or not, I had developed friendships with guys on and around the team—because they're good people, and it's impossible for me to shy from rooting for good people.

In addition, before I left Omaha in 2011, I met three of the eleven-member Peters family. I met mom Jenny, thirteen-year-old Charlie and two-year-old Teddy. I gave them a copy of the first book and explained that I would really like for Charlie to be part of the sequel, the story of the 2011 team.

To back up, I wrote a lot about Bayler Teal and his family in *Gamecock Glory*. Bayler, just seven years old, lost his battle with cancer during the 2010 series. Carolina played for him, won to honor him. As his dad Rob has said, it was a bittersweet story. It was sweet to see the impact of his life, but it was bitter to reckon with his death. It was easy to celebrate him, but it was hard to see him go.

Then came Charlie. In 2003, he had won his own bout with cancer. Years later, in 2011, he was South Carolina's batboy. That was incredible to me, in and of itself. Gamecocks coach Ray Tanner had reached out and befriended Charlie and his family eight years before, asking him to be part of the team. That says a lot about Tanner. He's genuine. His profile in South Carolina elevated a lot after the first title victory. He constantly had speaking engagements and functions to attend. Yet a year later, he was unafraid to slow down and include a teenage boy in what was going on with his team.

When I met Charlie and Jenny, I understood I had to write this book. I reminded myself of that throughout the rest of the summer and fall, even when I literally moved halfway across the country.

I cannot explain to you how special this family is; I recognized that in the short time I spent with the Peterses in June and November. I was thankful that Jenny, Matt, Morgan, Abby, Ben, Charlie, Max, Emma, Mae, Teddy and baby Zeke opened their home to me. (Yes, it's a rather large family.)

I've been really fortunate in recent years to meet people whose light emanates into the world around them, and Jenny Peters is one of those unique people, without question. She somehow holds together a house with nine kids on a daily basis. Even her husband, Matt, seems to struggle to explain how she does it with such vigor and positivity. It transcends admirable, really. If the world imitated her heart and kindness, man, it would be such a better place.

Charlie included, she instills that in her kids. Nine-year-old Emma and four-year-old Mae sent me personally designed Christmas cards, and they were the best presents I received—by far. Emma and Mae gave me a bag of candy when I left Omaha to return to Oklahoma City. They said she did not want me to fall asleep on my drive. Of course, Jenny is the driving force in the gifts and notes—the same as she was the driving force in Charlie making encouraging posters for South Carolina's baseball team.

So it's no wonder Charlie's such a good kid. And it's no wonder why I had to write this book. How could I not shine a light on a story like his, a family like that? They're so deserving, both the Gamecocks and the Peters family. They're so inspiring.

I cannot believe this is the third book I have completed in twelve months. I really cannot. It has been both exhausting and exhilarating, and I've been encouraged by so many who have enjoyed the work and the stories in these pages. Thank you for reading and providing that feedback; it's often been my fuel when I have struggled to juggle my day job and this project. This book, in so many ways, is my thank-you note to the Gamecocks faithfuls who adopted me as one of their own following the first title run. Your support and friendship means more to me than you will ever know.

No matter where I go, Carolina—and Columbia, specifically—will always be a home to me. And I sincerely thank you for that. None of this would have been possible if not for your passion and love for your hometown team. It was my pleasure working in the state for more than a half decade with the Anderson and Charleston newspapers.

I wish you all the very best. I wish, too, for continued success to Coach Tanner and his program.

I know the Gamecocks have sure put a lot of smiles on faces the past couple of years. I'm included.

Travis Haney
February 2012

P.S. And my thank-yous, of course. Thank you to God for blessing my life beyond all measure. To my parents for allowing me to dream big and giving me the means to make the dreams realities. To Drew, my very best friend, for being my very best friend in every season. To Mike and my patient and passionate editors at the *Oklahoman* for tolerating me while I finished yet another book about the Gamecocks. To Malcolm for hiring me in 2007 at the *Post and Courier* and opening the door for these adventures. To all those on or involved with the South Carolina baseball team who took the time to talk with me for this book. And to Michael Roth, in particular, for becoming a friend in the process of the past couple of years. I promise you that he'll do something big one day—and I doubt it will be in baseball. I could not have done this without any of you. It has been my honor and joy.

Taking Detours

One by one, they boarded the bus, adrenaline from the previous night's events the only fuel keeping them going. Hours earlier, South Carolina's baseball team had won the 2010 College World Series. In doing so, the Gamecocks had claimed the first major national championship ever won by the school in more than one hundred years of playing sports. It was the pinnacle of the coaches' and players' athletic lives and something celebrated—and celebrated some more—in the Palmetto State by millions of long-suffering fans whose patience had been pushed and pushed, to the point of surrender but never past it, for generations.

It was also significant in Omaha, Nebraska's largest city, because it was the final year for the College World Series to be played at venerable Rosenblatt Stadium. By 2011, the two-week summer festival would move a couple of miles away to a sparkling, state-of-the-art facility just north of downtown. There would be no champion after South Carolina at Rosenblatt, which was to be taken over by the adjacent zoo and turned into a park (and a parking lot).

Inside the bus, the Gamecocks were finally heading home on that Wednesday, the last day in June. Parties, even a parade down Main Street, were scheduled in Columbia once the heroes returned.

Not before a detour, however. Veteran coach Ray Tanner pulled the driver aside before the bus departed the team hotel. He asked him to turn left just before hitting the road to Eppley Airfield.

The charter wound up doing a loop around the construction site where work-in-progress TD Ameritrade Park was taking shape. Tanner did not go over the top with some type of grand speech, but he suggested that it would be nice to return to Omaha in 2011, to open the new park. At least one person on board jokingly rolled his eyes. "We just won a national title, and we're talking about next year already?" Gamecocks lead assistant coach Chad Holbrook recalled thinking.

The players, though, had a different reaction. They quickly went from tired to wired.

The confident, spirited statements rose up from different seats. The champions wanted more. They would have stormed off the bus right then and played on that pile of dirt if they could have.

"Yeah, let's open up the new place!"

"We'll be back next year!"

"Close down the old stadium, open the new one. Let's do it!"

Holbrook remembered smiling, taking a sip of coffee and wearily giving another roll of his eyes. "Those boys thought they could beat the New York Yankees that morning," he said. "It was a neat moment, but it was not a moment that for one minute made me think it was going to happen. But our kids did. 'It's going to be awesome to open that place up.' That was what they said. That was the conversation."

All Tanner and the players referenced, really, was returning. No one uttered a word about winning again. That's fair, right, after a century-long wait for the first one at South Carolina? Don't get too greedy, you know?

What the 2010 bunch had just proved, though, was that if you get to Omaha, you never know what might happen. The Gamecocks came through the losers' bracket to claim the first title, winning a College World Series–record six consecutive games after dropping the opener to Oklahoma. They staved off elimination four different times, including twice against rival Clemson. They were even down to their final strike in the twelfth inning against Oklahoma before pulling through with a miraculous victory to sustain their stay. South Carolina, returning for the first time since 2004, was unseeded but undaunted.

The 2011 team, nucleus intact, had that same fighting spirit. The Gamecocks turned Tanner's words into prophecy, enduring a number of injuries and hardships to advance to the College World Series at that new facility, TD Ameritrade Park.

They did okay once they arrived.

The 2011 season ended for South Carolina's baseball team just like the 2010 season had ended for South Carolina's baseball team. And it ended like so few seasons do in college sports or sports in general: with a victory, with a championship. It was not a bad way to go out, either, with fireworks glowing and popping in the summer sky and the Gamecocks launching their bodies toward one another to form the ceremonial dog pile.

It was a different stadium. It was mostly the same team. It was very much the same feeling. One of the newcomers to the celebration did not swing a bat or throw a pitch in the College World Series, but he certainly had every right to be there on that field.

As the players amassed to create a mound of human beings, a teenage boy stood to the side, sizing up the situation. He was looking for his point of entry to this fray. He wanted in.

Thirteen-year-old Charlie Peters first met Tanner and the Gamecocks in 2003, when he was lying in a hospital bed at Omaha's Children's Hospital. Turned out, this wasn't one of those stories in which an athletic team visits a sick kid and then shuffles along, impacted in the interim but not for any significant period of time. Something stuck with Tanner from that first encounter, Peters going toe to toe with cancer—and losing at the time. It stuck so profoundly that Tanner reached out, again and again, to stay in touch with the family.

The connection was kept alive long enough for Tanner and South Carolina's return to the College World Series in 2004. And, get this, Charlie had recovered by then. Tanner and the players were floored, humbled even, by his progress in a year's time.

The connection flickered, but it was sustained and remained when South Carolina, Tanner still in charge, finally made it back in 2010. "I was glad that they were coming back," Charlie said. "I hoped that the coach still remembered me."

Tanner did. After the team's opening loss to Oklahoma, and the realization that Charlie wasn't there, he invited the Peters clan—then ten strong, including eight kids—to the rest of the games. They were all Carolina wins, of course.

When the Gamecocks got back in 2011, Tanner had an idea: he asked Peters to be a batboy.

With Peters in the dugout, the Gamecocks were in the midst of living, breathing inspiration. They needed only to look at Charlie to understand there were bigger things in life than baseball. They had played with similar perspective and motivation in 2010, when Peters and his family sat in the stands at Rosenblatt. Additionally, South Carolina played for seven-year-old Bayler Teal, whose tangle with cancer unfortunately ended in the midst of the College World Series—during the middle of that dramatic game against Oklahoma. Bayler in death and Charlie in life, the Gamecocks were playing the past couple of years with something in their hip pockets that those other elite teams didn't have.

Finally, after sensing that he would not be crushed by the much larger baseball players, Peters went for it, flying into the pile. The child's smile, indelible, inched over his braces and shined on ESPN's TV cameras. What a moment, taking the emotions to their perfect and resounding crescendo. That was the snapshot. Click. Hold on to it in your mind forever, Charlie the cherry on top of the Gamecocks' dog pile—and season. What hope, to go from that hospital bed in 2003 to that baseball field in 2011.

The 2011 season ended for South Carolina's fans just like the 2010 season had ended for South Carolina's fans. Euphoria was again felt by fans of the team in attendance in Omaha and those at home who could not make it.

No one really knew what to do the first time. Spontaneous fits of joy filled the bars, homes and streets of Columbia. The joyous reaction was kind of similar on the Rosenblatt turf, too. But in 2011, it was familiar, a been-there, done-that sensation. It was a feeling, though, that in no way diminished the magnitude of what had just transpired. It was full-heartedly welcomed back by everyone in garnet and black.

The fact that South Carolina won in 2010 was surprising in the college baseball and athletic realms. The surprising part in 2011 was how the Gamecocks managed to repeat.

Surely they were toast from the start, losing weekend starters and Southeastern Conference veterans Blake Cooper and Sam Dyson. On top of that, even pitching coach Mark Calvi was gone. He had left to become the head-coach-in-waiting at South Alabama.

Pitching was the giant question, even with the bullpen anchored by All-America closer Matt Price, who blossomed during the first Omaha run. There was talent and promise, with a guy like junior left-hander Michael Roth headed for the weekend rotation, but that did not guarantee success.

The offense would lean heavily on sophomore first baseman Christian Walker and junior center fielder Jackie Bradley Jr., who were both postseason heroes from 2010. But who would produce consistently beyond that potent pair?

Injuries can never be projected—who or how many—but 2011 wound up being one of "those" years for the Gamecocks. "It almost got to the point that it was a joke," said starting outfielder Adam Matthews, who missed more than half the season with a nagging hamstring injury. "Every day, we'd come in and see who the next guy would be. It was like, 'Oh, OK, that's fine. We'll win anyway.'"

Win anyway. Handed down from Tanner, it was the team's mantra— something that carried through to the very end, even through the difficulty of losing Bradley, a preseason All-American and projected first-round draft pick, for an extended stretch with a wrist injury. Didn't matter, Tanner urged. Just win anyway.

The team played with the same gritty underdog mentality that had permeated in 2010, even though it was not technically much of an underdog in 2011. It's difficult to fly under the radar as a reigning national champ. That said, with the uncertainty about the pitching staff, the Gamecocks were picked to finish third—in their own division. A national title wasn't enough cachet to keep South Carolina from theoretically starting the season behind Florida and Vanderbilt. Not that that was completely offensive, considering how stocked both the Gators and Commodores were. No, more than sand in the eyes, it was an indication of how difficult the SEC's Eastern Division would be in 2011. Many expected those three teams— half the division—to reach Omaha. "I'd like to finish better than that," Tanner said before the season, "but I don't take that as any disrespect."

Florida was fielding essentially a minor-league team. Vanderbilt was doing about the same. Both were exceptionally deep and rich with pitching, and that's where pundits wondered about the Gamecocks.

South Carolina, though, liked being wondered about. The players relished being slighted, even going so far as to embellish the concept of disrespect as a motivational tool. "I don't think our team even wanted to be number one," Price said. "We knew we were good enough to be number one, but we wanted to beat number one more than we wanted to be number one."

At least until the end, anyway.

Chapter 1
Remaining Driven

R̲ay Tanner's mind intermittently raced during the months that followed the first national championship of his career. In between speaking engagements from one corner of the state to the other and beyond its borders, South Carolina's longtime head baseball coach often wondered about his team. Not the one that had just won, but the next one.

The Gamecocks had never before been champions. What went along with that? There was a curiosity on Tanner's part whether it would affect the chemical balance of each player and the team, collectively. How would the players respond in the off-season and once the 2011 season started?

Still sifting through those thoughts shortly after the team returned from Omaha, Tanner received a phone call. Louisiana State coach Paul Mainieri was on the other end of the line.

Mainieri's Tigers had won the national championship in 2009. In 2010, they limped into an NCAA Regional in Los Angeles and were subsequently knocked out by the University of California at Irvine, the Anteaters of UC–Irvine. Neither Mainieri nor Tanner had any way of knowing it at the time of their conversation, but LSU in 2011 would not even qualify for the eight-team Southeastern Conference Tournament, let alone the NCAA Tournament.

The talent level had dropped at LSU, for whatever reason, but Mainieri also noticed that winning the title had altered some of his players' attitudes. It had generally thrown off the group's equilibrium. It had affected focus and drive. As a friend and peer, Mainieri reached out to warn Tanner and perhaps prevent the Gamecocks from meeting a similar fate. "He helped me," Tanner said. "He helped prepare me for fall practice. He helped guard me against the celebration going on and on and on. I didn't want to take that away, but he helped me manage it."

Tanner conceived a message and had delivered it to his players by the time the fall semester began. At its heart, Tanner wanted to take the success of 2010 and the promise of 2011, throw them in a blender and spin them together. He did not want to eliminate the positives from 2010, but he also did not want the ever-present NCAA trophy to create a sense of relaxation and complacency in his players' psyches. "We can draw from the past, those things that give us strength and enable us to be better," Tanner recalled telling them, "but we can't dwell on it. We have to only draw from the good part that enables us to move forward."

The team seemed to understand. "He said this was a different team," junior pitcher Michael Roth said, then recalling some of Tanner's words. "'While some of you are national champions, you're not a national champion this year.'"

Tanner was calmed, as much as he is ever calmed, by what he saw during the fall practices. The players kept pushing one another. They kept working. No one was left with a residual feeling of comfort just because they had broken through to win big. Commanding and charismatic leadership, held over from the 2010 team, was urging the group forward. No one was caught looking at the shimmer of their rings. If someone began to get stagnant, lost in that daze, a teammate swiftly came along to shake him back to reality and the challenge of the new season.

"When we got back in the locker room for the fall, I went up to [closer Matt] Price and told him we had to stay hungry," said third baseman Adrian Morales, a rising senior who emerged in 2010 as a rock of a leader, a bad cop when one was needed. "He said, 'We will.' We knew we had to work to get back there. It wasn't just going to happen. And we knew we wanted to get back."

In some senses, a team is only as strong as its captains. When the 2011 captains were announced, just hours before the February 18 opener against Santa Clara, there was nothing more than a blink from fans and those inside the program. Roth, senior catcher Brady Thomas and senior second baseman Scott Wingo were all logically sound choices, all anticipated results from the team vote. They were veteran players who had made significant contributions to the 2010 title run. They were instrumental, each in his own way, in terms of developing the team's personality and makeup.

The 2011 University of South Carolina Baseball Team's Run to Back-to-Back NCAA Championships

Stepping back, though, it was kind of incredible how each one got to that day of distinction via individually winding roads. The three players were from the Upstate region of South Carolina, having competed against one another as youngsters, but there were few commonalities beyond that.

Roth had arrived at South Carolina with the hopes of being a run-producing power hitter in the middle of the Gamecocks' lineup. The only problem, albeit a rather large hurdle, was Roth's inability to hit or produce runs with any consistency. He struggled mightily to adapt to college pitching, so, naturally, he became a college pitcher—a join-'em-if-you-can't-beat-'em case of adaptation. Roth had thrown some in high school, and Mark Calvi, then the pitching coach, was in the market for a left-handed specialist.

Calvi's intuition paid off. Roth was dominant in the role, allowing three earned runs in twenty-four innings in the regular season. He had gone twenty-one appearances without allowing an earned run leading into the NCAA Tournament. Still, Roth wanted more than to face one or two batters. He wanted to be more involved. And in the College World Series, he received his wish.

The Gamecocks were thin all season when it came to starting pitching. So when they fell to the losers' bracket in Omaha, it forced Calvi to get creative. He turned to Roth to start an elimination game against rival Clemson because the Tigers featured a left-handed-heavy lineup and also, generally, because of Roth's competitive fire.

Calvi's intuition again paid off. Roth threw a complete-game three-hitter, stunning Clemson, to extend Carolina's stay. He started again, on three days' rest, and kept UCLA at bay for five innings in the game that ultimately ended with the Gamecocks holding a trophy. There are breakout performances, and then there's what Roth did. It was in a class of emergence all its own, pitching so well on the college sport's biggest stage.

Entering 2011, Tanner and new pitching coach Jerry Meyers knew that using Roth for twenty-four regular-season innings was not going to work. They thought he had the guile to be their Friday night starter, their ace. That part would require the season to prove or disprove; what they knew they could depend on was his ability to lead, pairing his fun-loving demeanor off the mound and his intensity when on it. Roth was as natural a captain as the team had.

Thomas was a viable choice, as well, if for no other reason than life experience. He left his hometown of Anderson to play at Florida State, which had been his dream since middle school. Thomas, though, wound up behind Buster Posey, an All-American who eventually became the number-five overall pick in the Major League Baseball draft.

Seeking playing time, Thomas left FSU and moved home. He was out of baseball and enrolled at a community college, getting his credits in order, when South Carolina's coaches invited him down for a visit. That visit turned into an offer to join the team.

To the studious Thomas, the strength of Carolina's nursing program meant just as much as the winning tradition of the baseball program. The classroom was initially more comfortable, too. In limited at-bats his first season in 2009, Thomas batted .174 in twenty-four games. He rebounded in 2010, hitting .331 in forty-seven games—second on the team to only Jackie Bradley Jr.—for the national champions.

What a way to go out, was what Thomas thought. He had already been on a college roster for five seasons. But Tanner suggested that Thomas ask the NCAA for a sixth year, based on a medical condition he had dealt with during his freshman year at FSU. Thomas was initially denied the extra year by the NCAA, but he learned two weeks before the 2011 season that he would in fact be eligible to play.

It was a happy ending to a trying few months, which were made more difficult by the fact that Thomas was not even allowed to practice or work out with the team. Just like that, he was right back in the fold. "It was probably one of the best feelings I've ever had," Thomas said of the day when the coaching staff delivered the good news and told him to grab his gear for practice. Being named a captain was sweet icing on the treat of a sixth year, a stay of his college career.

As for Wingo, it seemed as if he had been on campus for a decade. He had started at second base from day one, becoming a staple in the Gamecocks' middle infield. He might not have been a structured and cerebral leader, like Roth and Thomas were, but Wingo was perhaps the most likeable guy on the team. He would make you laugh. He would make you shake your head. The contrast of a heart of gold and mischief in his eyes, he was the consummate little brother.

In addition to an infectious personality, he also had a dogged work ethic that earned him respect from his peers and coaches. Still, there was room for growth. Wingo had been a steady, slick fielder his first three years, but the bat had not cooperated. He had a career .226 average heading into his final season at Carolina. He vowed to change his approach in 2011, and his teammates, with their vote as evidence, believed he would adjust to become a more all-around player as a senior. They were more correct than they knew, really.

Roth, Thomas and Wingo would lead the Gamecocks into a new season, the first title defense in South Carolina's history.

The 2011 University of South Carolina Baseball Team's Run to Back-to-Back NCAA Championships

After a particularly cold winter in Columbia—it even snowed twice—the 2011 season finally arrived at Carolina Stadium. So did the sun. It was seventy-five degrees and distinctly beautiful for the February 18 opener against Santa Clara.

Reminders of what had been accomplished the previous year were everywhere. Among the fresh décor was a giant mural on the back side of the center field batter's eye. Snapshots from the first championship season were plastered high and large on it for everyone to see upon entering the stadium's main gates. There were images such as Whit Merrifield's title-winning hit, Bradley accepting the College World Series' Most Outstanding Player trophy—and, of course, the dog pile.

A flag commemorating the championship was raised just before the first pitch as a quartet of fighter jets roared over the stadium for what very well might have been the first flyover at a regular-season college baseball game.

Celebrating was natural, a given. There were myriad reasons to do so. But, in line with Tanner's concerns, would it have an impact on the team? Would the players be so caught up in looking back that they would lose sight of the present and immediate future? Winning in 2010 would guarantee nothing in 2011. Could the Gamecocks avoid the propensity to let off the accelerator a bit, keep from coasting on their previous merits?

Tanner's message at least seemed as if it had taken hold. With the literal and metaphorical fireworks going off all around them on Opening Day, the players were saying the right things. "We can't be complacent," said Bradley, a preseason All-America center fielder. "We've got to put everything in the past behind us. Everybody knows 'championship this' and 'championship that,' but what you do coming up isn't related to what you did last year."

If one day was any indication, South Carolina was going to be just fine. It blew past Santa Clara 12–5, getting home runs from Bradley and Christian Walker. Bradley went 4 for 4 on the day, picking up where he had left off in Omaha.

Still, it was just one game. There were more than sixty to go.

"The truth of the matter is, it is time to turn the page," Tanner said then. "It's a great memory, and it's okay to draw from it, but from this point forward we're going to try to do the best we can to put a good club on the field in 2011."

Chapter 2
Stoking Fires

Michael Roth had his left hand on the wheel and the other feeling around for his Carolina Stadium parking pass when he heard the crunch. The junior winced, realizing he had rear-ended the car in front of him. It was not the best start to a day, much less one in which he was scheduled to pitch—and especially one in which he was to go against rival Clemson. The last time the Tigers had seen Roth, he had mesmerized them for nine innings in the College World Series. It was the first of two Carolina wins in two days to put the Gamecocks in the national championship series—and send Clemson home.

Before his follow-up performance against the Tigers, first Roth had to get to the stadium. The woman whose car he hit was not terribly upset. The highway patrolman was pleasant; he told Roth he was excited to meet him. Still, Roth had a routine that was being upset, even if it was his fault. "It was enough to piss me off," he said. "I was late. I missed the team meal."

Fortunately, a teammate saved him a plate. As he ate, Roth tried to rid himself of the bad energy and mentally prepare himself for what was ahead. "Once I got on the field, all those feelings left," he said. "When it's Clemson, everything goes to a whole other level. We want to go out there and destroy them. That's the feeling you get once you're here for a couple of years." He laughed. "Or even a couple of days."

So the contentious feelings were evident in both dugouts, with Clemson seeking revenge and Carolina harboring familiar contempt. The tension was often thick for the rivalry, which was first played in 1899, but there was something uniquely intense about the March 4 meeting, the first of the teams' three-game series. With both fan bases represented for a Friday night game, it was one of the more raucous environments in the four-year history of Carolina Stadium.

The tension went up a notch—or two or three—in the third inning when Clemson outfielder Jeff Schaus was caught in a rundown between first and second base. It ended with Roth, who was covering first base, applying a hard tag under Schaus's right ear. He essentially punched Schaus in the jaw with his glove. Schaus popped up and heatedly said something to Roth. Roth responded with a few choice words as he walked back to the mound. "That's just the Clemson rivalry at its finest," he said later, laughing. Carolina second baseman Scott Wingo, whose father was a star at Clemson in the 1970s, was the closest player to the tag. "It got heated quick, didn't it?" he said.

Roth was 2-0 at the time, but the wins were against Santa Clara and Southern Illinois. This was his first major test since the last time he had seen Clemson. He wanted to prove that the complete game was no fluke and that the Gamecocks could count on him as a big-game anchor, just as they had with Blake Cooper in 2010. The captain did just that. Clemson scored three unearned runs in the top of the second, but Roth and the Carolina bullpen held the Tigers scoreless thereafter. Roth lasted seven innings, giving up three hits—just like Omaha—while striking out six.

Closer Matt Price went the final 1⅔ innings, striking out three of the five batters he faced, to pick up his third save in four appearances and seal a 6–3 Carolina victory. The Gamecocks had a perfect 8-0 record after the win to gain the early advantage in the series. Two-run home runs by Brady Thomas and Wingo—the other two captains—and first baseman Christian Walker provided the offense.

The day ended a lot better for Roth than it had begun. Suddenly, a dented fender did not seem so bad. "Overall, I'd say it's a great day because we beat Clemson," he said that night. "I'll just have to get the car fixed."

Walker's home run, with two outs in the fifth inning, ultimately wound up being the game-winner Friday at Carolina Stadium. With fourteen runs batted in and three home runs in the team's first eight games, the sophomore first baseman was on a tear to begin the season. He was batting .552 (16 for 29) entering the second game of the Clemson series.

That was particularly prodigious production relative to the much-ballyhooed new bats in college baseball. They were still made of metal, but the composition had been refined to adhere to the NCAA's newly adopted Ball-Bat Coefficient of Restitution (BBCOR) standard. Simply put, the formula of metals was altered to reduce the spring effect of the bat. The bats had a similar look but a completely different sound when they met the ball. The stinging *ping* sound was replaced by more of a hollow *thud*.

In action, the results figured to resemble the wood bat used in professional baseball. The expectation was that home runs would still be hit but at a far lower rate. Some, pitching purists, excitedly said this would be the death of the 12–10 college baseball game. Others, fans of offense, said it would be the end of excitement at ballparks across the country. They said the homers were a means of attracting fans.

Judging by the Friday night win against Clemson, the Gamecocks missed the memo about the power outage. Their three home runs seemed to indicate that Carolina would continue to knock the ball out of the park. After Saturday's neutral-site game in Greenville was rained out and rescheduled for the following Tuesday, the Gamecocks resumed their home run derby Sunday afternoon in Clemson. The bats, talked about to no end early in the year, again took center stage during the game, though for a different reason.

Walker hit his fourth home run, his third in three games, to lead off the seventh inning. Earlier, in the first inning, Jackie Bradley Jr. hit his third home run of the season. The Gamecocks' 3 and 4 hitters were sizzling. As Bradley's teammates congratulated him, Clemson coach Jack Leggett trotted out to speak with home plate umpire Randy Harvey.

Leggett wanted Harvey to check Bradley's bat, which was hot to the touch when a Clemson player picked it up. Puzzled expressions filled the South Carolina dugout. "Our bats were in the sun," Roth said. "We were told to move them out of the sun. We were like, 'Is he serious? Is this guy joking?' We were kind of laughing about it. We kind of thought it was funny, that they were going to have to go to call us cheaters, and all that, to win a ballgame."

Bradley's bat was deemed permissible, and the home run counted. The gamesmanship, or whatever Leggett's reasoning was, incensed the Gamecocks. Coach Ray Tanner said it was the only time in his career that his team had been accused of cheating, even though there was nothing in the rulebook about heating bats (naturally with sunlight or artificially with a warming sleeve). "Coach Tanner would do nothing to jeopardize the integrity of the game," Roth said. "We would do nothing to compromise the integrity of the game. We didn't think we were cheating or even breaking the rules. We felt like we were just being resourceful."

It is difficult to say whether Leggett's move affected the Gamecocks, but Clemson did win 10–5. Aided by Walker's home run, South Carolina pushed across four runs in the seventh to take a 5–3 lead. But the Tigers shelled Price in the eighth, knocking him around for 6 earned runs in two-thirds of an inning. It was Price's worst outing of the season, by far. With the sun and temperature dipping as he took the mound, he really had no command of his pitches. He gave up four hits and walked two, just two days after pitching perfectly for the five-out save in Columbia.

As if it had not been a long enough day for the Gamecocks, they later learned that Clemson's Will Lamb had sounded off after the game. Asked about a walk, Lamb took a shot at Carolina starter Tyler Webb, calling him "soft." That sent the Gamecocks over the edge, especially considering they initially thought Lamb was referring to Price, maybe the gutsiest player on the team. "It doesn't matter who it is about," Roth said on Twitter. "You call one of us out, you call all of us out."

Tanner added to that Monday during an appearance on a Columbia radio station. "I don't think there's a place in the game for any of those kinds of comments," he said. "Sometimes young people say things they shouldn't say. In this case, if he said it, I would advise against it."

With a day between the second and third games in the series, due to the rainout, there was plenty of time for the Gamecocks to stew. "They really got to us," said Price, from Sumter. "It just made the rivalry more intense, more competitive. It's like there was more anger between us."

South Carolina was one irritated baseball team on that Monday, the day before the rubber game against Clemson in Greenville. The agitation was audible when assistant coach Chad Holbrook did his weekly radio stint with 107.5 "The Game" in Columbia. Holbrook told hosts Jay Philips and Michael Haney:

Maybe Clemson needs to be asked what the problem was. All I know is it never has been a part of anything going on. You can't do anything to these bats. You try like crazy to keep them as warm as you can. You don't want them cold. There's nothing, anything, written down anywhere, whatsoever, that [says] keeping the bat in the sunlight makes the bat perform better.

I really don't know what the accusation was. I can assure you there's nothing—never has been, never will be—anything from a rules-breaking standpoint going on in our dugout.

Some of the players, who were using Twitter more and more, vented on the social medium. "I love our bats," said Bradley, the player Leggett asserted had homered with a hot bat. For good measure, Bradley added a smiley face.

Tanner decided to hold an afternoon practice to keep everyone fresh and let them blow off some of the collecting steam. First, though, he met with the players. He gave them a forum to talk about what had happened during and after the loss at Clemson. It was the only time Tanner recalled having to address an opposing player's comments. He said:

I think they expected me to be a little more outspoken about it than I had been at that point. You know how we are as coaches. We take the high road a lot of times. I tried to express that in a nice way. I asked how they felt. They asked how I felt. And, truthfully, I felt similarly to them, but I wasn't going to say anything.

We sort of talked it over. The players pushed some of the responsibility to me. They said, "If we can't express ourselves, then we'd like for you to do it for us." I thought that was fair.

Tanner told them he would publicly make his feelings known, on one condition: they had to win the next night. The players roared. It was a deal.

In the interim, Tanner did throw the team a bone. Roth said Tanner told the players they could have "free rein" to heckle the Tigers in the deciding game. "You can say whatever you want," Roth recalled Tanner saying. "I want you to be all over them." The Gamecocks liked the sound of that. By the second inning, they had already been warned by the umpiring crew to tone it down. Roth remembered Tigers outfielder Chris Epps, amazed by what he was hearing, looking strangely into the Carolina dugout as he ran to first base. "We felt like we were already in their heads," Roth said.

That was not evident, necessarily, on the Fluor Field scoreboard. It was a tight, low-scoring game—just the type of game that the new bats had promised. Clemson led 1–0 through six and a half innings when the Gamecocks, then into the Tigers bullpen, finally found some offense. A Peter Mooney infield single tied the game and left runners on first and second with one out. Tanner told Roth to grab a bat, with the idea that he would pinch-hit against right-handed reliever Alex Frederick. Roth was never announced, though, and Tanner instead sent Jake Williams to the plate when left-hander Joseph Moorefield came in to pitch. Williams launched Moorefield's 0-1 pitch over the wall in left-center field. The Wofford transfer's three-run shot, one of his two home runs all season, put the Gamecocks ahead 4–1. The South Carolina contingent, and those in the dugout, went bonkers.

After 2⅓ innings in relief of starter Adam Westmoreland, freshman Forrest Koumas ran out of gas, and Carolina needed Price to put out a fire in the top of the ninth. The Tigers had scored three runs to cut the lead to 5–4. Lamb, of all people, stood on third base, representing the tying run. While at that station, bulldog Adrian Morales gave Lamb an earful. As Morales continued to jabber in his direction, Lamb appeared as meek as the animal that shares his name. Price struck out pinch hitter Jon McGibbon to end the game, leaving Lamb on third. It was the team's second of an impressive thirteen victories in one-run games.

Sure enough, Tanner was good to his word. In the postgame media session, Tanner let Leggett and the Tigers know what was on his mind. "I didn't appreciate it. I'm offended by it. I don't cheat," Tanner told reporters. "I don't allow my players to cheat. We haven't done anything wrong. I felt like we were called out a little bit. I don't appreciate what Will Lamb said about one of my pitchers. I just don't think what happened is appropriate. It's not what this rivalry is about."

The players might have been happier about Tanner's uncharacteristic outburst than the win itself. They took to Twitter that night, making jokes about their coach being more imposing than cult hero Chuck Norris. The Gamecocks had picked up a big series win against Clemson, then ranked fourth in the country, but they also bonded over what Tanner angrily called the Tigers' "shenanigans." "I definitely think that showed our coach is behind our back 100 percent," Wingo said. "It showed he cares for and about us. I always knew he had, but it showed."

Tanner said he made up with Leggett about a week later. "When two human beings, regardless of their relationship—when you have a chance to express how you really feel, both people might say things that aren't liked," Tanner said. "But you both feel better that you were able to get it out. Before we hung up, I think we got it resolved."

Chapter 3
Erasing Errors

When it comes to personalities, it's difficult to get any more of a spectrum than from South Carolina's shortstop in 2010 to South Carolina's shortstop in 2011. Bobby Haney was the brash, sharp-tongued New Yorker, the life of really any party. His departure opened the door for Peter Mooney, an extremely quiet kid from South Florida, someone you would almost forget were present if you weren't looking directly at him.

For their differences, Haney and Mooney had one basic similarity: they had reputations as outstanding fielders, terribly important for what is known as the most difficult defensive position in baseball. Haney fielded and threw cleanly 97.6 percent of the time his senior season, incredible for a shortstop. With Haney leading, the team fielded at a .975 clip, which put it in the top third of the country.

Coaches Ray Tanner and Chad Holbrook felt as if they had found an able replacement in Mooney, who won a junior college Gold Glove both years he was at Palm Beach Community College.

Haney and Mooney were similar, too, in that it took time for them to settle once they made the jump from JUCO ball to the Southeastern Conference. Haney committed eleven errors his junior season, his first after transferring in from Manatee Community College on Florida's Gulf Coast. He cut that nearly in half, to six, the next year. In 2010, eight of his eleven errors came in a span from April 7 to May 14, in the middle of the conference stretch run.

Mooney's difficulties surfaced earlier, hitting their peak during the March 18 SEC opener, a home game against Georgia. A first-inning throwing error on Mooney, his seventh error in sixteen games, led to Georgia's second run in a 4–2 victory. Mooney, who had committed just four errors the previous season in a competitive junior college league, was on pace for thirty in his first year at South Carolina.

It wasn't just Mooney that night against the Bulldogs; the Gamecocks had a Tanner era–high five errors in the loss. But Mooney, the younger brother of former Florida infielder Mike Mooney, had become representative of the issues. He admitted later in the season that he was "stressing himself" to live up to his fielding hype. "I was not comfortable," Mooney said. "I was having a hard time. That was supposed to be my strong point. I don't really know what was going on defensively."

Mooney's defense was affecting his offense, too. In that Georgia loss, he struck out three times in four at-bats. Tanner saw Mooney's expression sinking on and off the field. Some fans booed after his first-inning error, what was his third of the week and second in as many games. After the game, Tanner invited Mooney into his office to assess his confidence level and whether it needed to be reconstructed.

"That was not me at all," Mooney said, laughing nervously. "Things were just not going my way then and there. Coach met with me after that game. We talked it over and he was like, 'Listen, I know things haven't gone your way. You've got to let that go. It's a new season tomorrow.' From that point on, I feel like I turned it on."

Mooney still committed seven more errors in 2011, but he made a lot more spectacular plays—often teaming up with second baseman Scott Wingo—than miscues. Mooney and Wingo would turn out to be a highlight machine during the College World Series. That would not have happened if Mooney had lost faith back in March. "His nerves were going there," Wingo said. "He had growing pains, I guess. He got through that quick. He didn't say much, just kept playing and got through it."

It had been a trying week, really, after a home loss to Cal State Bakersfield and a road loss at Furman—paired with the loss to the Bulldogs—dropped Carolina to 12-4. The Gamecocks, mind you, did not lose a midweek game during the entire 2010 season, and they had dropped two in a row as they approached the SEC season. And then they lost the conference opener, needing wins on that Saturday and Sunday to avoid an SEC series loss to start league play.

Put simply, South Carolina needed a win. For the first time in the 2011 season, it would lean on Wingo to get that win. It was the first time, but not the last time, that Wingo would prove to be a savior as a senior.

There were tense times, every now and again, when it came to Tanner and Wingo's relationship. That is a Tanner thing, really: lean hard on the players when they're younger and then gradually loosen up as they mature and progress toward their potential. Wingo, despite being named a captain, still had remaining gears entering his senior season. His glove at second base had been a constant, exemplary; his bat had been an enigma.

Wingo hit .230 his freshman year. "I thought, 'That wasn't awful,'" he said. "I hit six home runs. I thought it was something to build on. I thought I was just getting settled. I thought I was weak, getting into the weight room for the first time, really." His expectations were higher for his sophomore season. But he hit .196, worst among the team's starters by nearly 100 points. "I was like, 'What the heck?' I was struggling."

In his postseason evaluation, Tanner leveled with Wingo. He was going to have to recruit someone else to play second base. Playing solid defense was not enough to keep him in the lineup. Wingo's head initially dropped, but then the plucky player met Tanner in the eyes. "That's fine," he said, "but I'm going to work hard and win that spot."

Tanner thought it sounded nice enough, bold enough, but there was nothing to indicate that Wingo would actually do that. Tanner was going off Wingo's track record, looking at two years to the contrary. Really, could he improve? Was that reasonable?

Nothing had changed by the time fall practice began. Tanner told Wingo he would be a bench player as a junior, a utility guy who would come in as a late-inning defensive replacement. Wingo fumed. "What are you talking about?" he asked, snapping at Tanner. He again told Tanner he would win the job. Tanner's jaw clenched, and he said, "All right." Wingo homered that day in his first at-bat of the first fall scrimmage.

Wingo had his rises and falls as a junior, initially making progress at the plate before a leg injury brought back some poor hitting habits. Wingo was benched to begin the NCAA Tournament, but he did enough—as the school's all-time hit-by-pitches leader, he always found ways to get on base—to play during the important super regional and College World Series games. The fact was, the Gamecocks were not as good without Wingo's glove. The alternatives weakened the team more than his inability to hit.

But 2010 really was about one moment for Scott Wingo. Forget the .247 batting average, still worst among starters. Forget the .963 fielding percentage, his catapult to the SEC's All-Defensive Team. The fact that Wingo scored the run to win the national title is what cemented him in Gamecocks lore. Whit Merrifield created one indelible image, his tongue hanging out and arms raised as he jogged to first. Wingo created another behind him, helmet flying off as he went from third to home in a dead sprint, meeting his jubilant teammates once he touched the plate. "That's going to live forever," Tanner said of the moment. "That's something extremely special."

So why not build off it? Wingo considered that, ramping up his off-season workout plan, specifically paying attention to the legs that had betrayed him in 2010. His plate approach changed, too, with Holbrook's help. Wingo recognized he had been far too pull-happy, trying to hit home runs, and he needed to work the ball more to left and center fields. "I was there in the cages with him," said senior third baseman Adrian Morales, one of the players once recruited to replace Wingo at second base. "I saw the work he was doing. You have to get to a point where you stop hitting in batting practice like it's a home run derby."

The season was exactly a month old, but Wingo had already posted a share of mixed results by the start of the 2011 SEC schedule. He called his start at the plate "okay" before he went into a spiral that dropped his average to .205 by the week of the Georgia series. A here-we-go-again feeling was setting in with Wingo and his coaches.

On top of that, his captaincy had to some extent been smeared by the comical-yet-not-funny fact that he missed the bus to Greenville for the third and final game against Clemson. Months later, Wingo was still ashamed to admit he was asleep when the team left for that monumentally big early season game. Exacerbating the dilemma, Wingo is from the Greenville suburb of Mauldin. His dad, Bill, was an outstanding player at Clemson in the 1970s. It wasn't Wingo's finest hour, to be sure. It was the anti–Omaha 2010. "I want to forget that," he said. "That's unreal. That's just pitiful." The phone call to Tanner, telling him why he had missed the bus, was rather unpleasant. "No, that wasn't fun. He was mad, man."

Tanner put Wingo's fate in the hands of the other two captains, pitcher Michael Roth and catcher Brady Thomas. The options: Wingo could start that night and be suspended the following five games, leading up to the Georgia series. Or he could sit that night and suffer no further punishment. Wingo wanted to play. It was Clemson, he reasoned. He thought he could call Tanner's bluff—well, if he were bluffing. "Just tell him to give me the five games," Wingo told his fellow captains. "Hopefully he won't really mean that."

Roth and Thomas decided that losing Wingo for five games would be more of a detriment to the team. "I felt awful," Wingo said. "My last game against Clemson, and I didn't even start." Tanner did compromise, allowing Wingo to enter the game as a defensive replacement. But still, the embarrassing episode was reported before the game.

Among the things to note about Wingo is his resiliency. It is incredibly difficult, and perhaps impossible, to keep him down. So despite his sinking batting average and his bus misstep, Wingo again bounced back. In the late innings on March 19, Wingo's season began in earnest. His average never went below .268 the rest of the season, and he stayed above .300 after April 7.

Carolina and Georgia were tied at one going into the bottom of the ninth, which started with consecutive singles from Morales and Jake Williams, the hero from the Clemson game. Morales stood at third, and Williams at second, by the time Wingo reached the plate with two outs.

In one of those dramatic situations dreamed about on Little League fields across the country, the count was full and the winning run was ninety feet away in the bottom of the ninth. Perhaps the fantasy most often ends with a home run, but an infield hit works, too. Wingo bounced a ground ball between first and second base, and Georgia first baseman Jonathan Hester made an athletic play to keep it in front of him. He popped up and flipped the ball underhand to pitcher Patrick Boling. By the time Boling got over to cover the base, though, Wingo was sliding headfirst across it, and Morales had scored the winning run.

Wingo scrambled to his feet and immediately spiked his helmet like a football, posing with a put-on scowl until his teammates arrived to greet him. The goat for missing the bus twelve days earlier, Wingo was now a hero. It was his first walk-off hit of the season. And there would be others.

With the Gamecocks riding the high from Wingo's hit, Georgia never had a chance in the Sunday rubber game. They scored in five of the eight innings in which they had an at-bat on the way to an 8–3 series-clinching victory. Wingo was on base four times, including a pair of hits. Led by outfielder Adam Matthews's 3-for-3 day, the team had seven players register a hit.

Freshman right-hander Forrest Koumas continued to make a case for a starting role. He gave up one run in 3⅓ innings, striking out six, to get his second victory out of the bullpen.

The Gamecocks had avoided the opening-series loss with victories in consecutive days, but the test was about to get tougher: number-one Florida was next on the SEC schedule.

Chapter 4
Proving Mettle

As much fun as the 2010 and 2011 Gamecocks liked to have—illustrated, for instance, by an in-game Rockettes routine performed in the bullpen by the relievers—there was another side to the team. It did not like to be doubted, so much that it actually became either accustomed or addicted, or both, to the boulder on its shoulder. South Carolina played better as an underdog, with the 2010 postseason serving as the shining example. The team eventually preferred that role.

The Gamecocks did not understand how they could win a national title, return as much as they did and not be the number-one-ranked team entering the following year. In reality, they started third due to pitching concerns and the relative strength of SEC East foes Florida and Vanderbilt. But it was no matter in the Carolina clubhouse. "What do we have to do?" was the common refrain.

That attitude had not changed by March 25, when the Gamecocks traveled to play top-ranked Florida in Gainesville. The Gators, the preseason number one, were 18-2 and had just swept then number-eight Louisiana State on the road. They were stocked with future Major Leaguers, loaded in particular with pitchers such as Hudson Randall and Karsten Whitson. Catcher Mike Zunino went on in 2011 to become the league's most valuable offensive player. "There aren't any weaknesses," Ray Tanner said that week of the Gators. "You have to dig really, really deep to find anything. I haven't found them."

Carolina, ranked fourth, was 14-4 and had lost to Furman and Georgia the previous week. Really, it was completely justified for the teams to be where they were. Still, that edginess was present entering the weekend. "Anytime we faced a number-one team, we wanted to beat them to prove we were still the best," ace Michael Roth said. "We wanted to prove we were defending our title."

Adding to it, the Gamecocks had not forgotten about the way the 2010 regular season closed. The Gators were in Columbia for the final SEC series. The winner of the best-of-three would claim the conference title. Florida did, winning two intense, close games. The second, on Senior Day at Carolina Stadium, ended with the Gators celebrating on the Gamecocks' field.

They thought, too, that their home environment—their fans—should earn them some credit in the polls. Carolina Stadium regularly sold out, and it averaged 7,390 fans a game in 2011—among the national leaders. As much as Florida is known for the hostility and raucousness of its football stadium, the Swamp, support for the baseball program has typically lagged, despite great spring weather and successful teams. "Fans don't show up, even when they are number one," Roth said. "I wanted to win the series, just to kind of prove a point. While they had all these stud guys, we were still a good team."

Roth had the ball in the opener, attempting to make that point known. It was his biggest start since the Clemson series and his first since the loss, his first, a week earlier to Georgia. Like that Clemson start, Roth was up for the challenge. He pitched into the ninth inning for the first time in 2011, holding a Florida offense batting .328 to a pair of runs.

Meanwhile, the offense—in full bloom that week—came to his aid. The Gamecocks had been scuffling through mid-March until an explosion of forty-one combined runs in the midweek wins against the College of Charleston and Rhode Island. Outfielder Adam Matthews drove in 8 runs, homering twice, in the 24–4 win against Charleston. Preseason All-American Jackie Bradley Jr. went hitless in his previous nineteen at-bats, slipping to an unBradley-like .288 average, before rallying with a three-hit game and a home run against the Cougars. Bradley homered again the next night, scoring three runs and driving in two more, in a 17–8 blasting of Rhode Island.

The potency at the plate continued against the country's top-rated team. Florida starter Brian Johnson was knocked around for 7 runs, including 6 earned, in 5⅓ innings. Jake Williams hit the second of his two home runs on the season. The Wofford transfer picked his moments, helping the team with homers against Clemson and Florida. Williams and Peter Mooney each had three hits. Each starter in the lineup had at least one hit, in fact. The 9–2 victory was a thorough beating on enemy turf.

"We made a statement," Roth said.

That statement would not mean a whole lot, however, if the Gamecocks could not find a way to get another win in the next two days to claim the series. Complicating that, the starting pitching beyond Roth had gone from a question mark in the preseason to several question marks by the end of the season's first full month. It was the first real dilemma for Jerry Meyers, back for his second stint as Carolina's pitching coach.

After three consecutive College World Series appearances with the Gamecocks, Meyers left in 2004 to become the head coach at Old Dominion. He still spoke weekly, or close to it, with Tanner, comparing notes and catching up with his old friend. Meyers recalled watching South Carolina's games on television when he was on the road with his team. He caught a couple of the games in Omaha as well. "I was keeping pretty close tabs," he said.

So when Mark Calvi left to become the head-coach-in-waiting at South Alabama, did Meyers even internally entertain the idea of a return? "I'd be lying to you if I said it didn't enter my mind," he said, "but it wasn't something I necessarily thought was going to happen." Tanner brought up the job to Meyers during one of their normal, casual conversations, but even then, Meyers was not sure if a second tour of duty at Carolina was the right thing.

Old Dominion had just hired a new athletic director, Camden Wood Selig, and he had vowed to make a deeper commitment to Meyers and the baseball program. As part of that, Meyers had just agreed to a new five-year deal. Tanner did not have to beg, though. The pull of being part of a winner at the highest level dwarfed having his own team. Meyers was back in the familiar garnet and black by August 2010. "I never really thought I would come back," he said. "I never thought that would be in the plans. I guess something deep down made you think about it, wondering if it happened again how it might go. I would not have guessed it would unfold like that, but things happen for a reason."

Meyers said his family missed living in Columbia. And he missed coaching in Omaha after getting three different tastes of it—and coming within a win of the title in 2002. He had missed the breakthrough in 2010, but he did not want to miss the next opportunity. If the Gamecocks were going back in 2011, it would be in large part up to Meyers, who was working to extract the best from several unproven arms.

Freshman Forrest Koumas certainly fit underneath that umbrella. Getting more long relief opportunities, including his victory the previous weekend against Georgia, the right-hander was showing a level of competitiveness that intrigued the coaches. Meyers, though, was not sure if he had enough command to become a starter in his first year. He often hit batters. He was falling behind in counts a bit too much. But he had still earned a shot in a rotation that had seen Tyler Webb, Adam Westmoreland and Steven Neff stumble due to inconsistencies and mild injuries.

Koumas would get the Saturday start at Florida because there were very few options at that point. (Tanner and Meyers could not even venture a guess for Sunday's starter and didn't, really, until Sunday morning.) Koumas's counterpart for his first college start? The best pitcher in the league in 2011—beyond Roth, anyway. Randall, a sophomore, finished the year 11-3 with a 2.17 ERA. He baffled the Gamecocks in one of his two complete games of the season. He gave up one unearned run on five hits, did not walk anyone and struck out four.

A Kamm Washington solo home run off closer Matt Price in the seventh inning was the difference. Meyers and Tanner vowed to use Price in tight situations, even if they came earlier than the ninth inning. Price had performed well in those sorts of appearances in Omaha in 2010, going between 1⅔ and 3 innings in his four College World Series appearances for a total of 9⅔ innings.

Price threw Washington a first-pitch fastball in the seventh, and Washington got enough metal on it to send the pitch out to left-center. With Randall throwing the way he was, that was enough for a 2–1 Florida victory to even the series and force Carolina's second SEC rubber game in as many weekends.

More significant than what Randall did, impressive as it was, was what Koumas did to stick with him. He went six innings, giving up an unearned run on two hits, while walking two and striking out five. He did hit three Gators, but the low hit count sufficed to balance out the number of base runners. Meyers had seen enough. The Gamecocks lost the game, but they had gained a starter. "He learned a lot that day," Meyers said. "We learned a lot that day."

Saturday behind him, Meyers then tried to figure out the Sunday pitching dilemma.

That Sunday for the Gamecocks was what is known in baseball as a Johnny Wholestaff game. Get an inning here from one guy, inning there from another, piece it together and hope you are still in striking distance at the end of the day.

That's far from ideal anytime but especially when facing one of the best teams in the country in a game to decide the series. Florida had its pitching set; no question about that. It would throw Whitson, who had turned down $2.1 million from the San Diego Padres to be a Gator. So, no, it was not ideal, but what choice did the Gamecocks have? Say "oh well" and go home, forfeit the final game?

Koumas had been a pleasant surprise in Saturday's game. Meyers was hopeful of the same Sunday from left-hander Bryan Harper, a first-year junior college transfer.

The older brother of Bryce Harper, the top pick in the 2010 Major League draft, had arrived at Carolina with high expectations—probably in part because of his sibling's prodigious reputation. The early season results had not really been overly spectacular, and Harper was something of a curious choice to begin the deciding game. Then again, a similar situation in Omaha had led the coaching staff to Roth. That worked out. Why couldn't Harper?

This experiment did not, though. It turned out to be the first and only start of Harper's one-year career with the Gamecocks. He lasted just two innings against the Gators, giving up a season-high three runs on three hits and a walk.

Things were bleak. After the second inning, Carolina trailed by three runs on the road against the top team in the country. Sophomore Colby Holmes, who had started the previous Tuesday in the walloping of Charleston, was next on the mound.

The three scoreless innings he came up with, giving up a hit and walking three, steadied the team and allowed it an opportunity to crawl back into the game—and series. It was not on the same level as Koumas's start, but it gave Meyers similar feelings about the future of the rotation. Holmes had been establishing himself in the midweek role, but perhaps he was ready for a move to SEC competition. Like Koumas, he had at least earned a chance. "We went into that weekend with some question marks about what we were going to be able to do," Meyers said. "I don't know that it was a turning point, but we left there going, 'All right, we've got a little better feeling about what we've got for next week.'"

The strong pitching performance had still resulted in a loss on Saturday, and if the bats didn't resurface it was going to happen again Sunday. But

The 2011 University of South Carolina Baseball Team's Run to Back-to-Back NCAA Championships

South Carolina had some remaining energy. It sent six batters to the plate in the sixth inning. The Gamecocks had just one hit, but they scored three runs. A fielding error on Nolan Fontana, one of the best shortstops in the country, was vital in continuing the inning. Tied 3–3, Carolina was back in the game—another close one.

Matthews, still scorching at the plate, led off the eighth inning with a double in the right-center field gap. A hit batter, a sacrifice bunt, an intentional walk and an unintentional walk of Adrian Morales pushed Matthews across the plate with the go-ahead run.

Price redeemed himself for Saturday's loss, pitching the final 2⅓ innings—including a strikeout of Washington in the eighth—to win his second game of the season. Holmes, John Taylor and Price pitched the final 7 innings without allowing a run. It was the definition of a team victory, though the Gamecocks—especially once injuries hit in bulk—would continually redefine that concept as the season continued.

One downside of the win was that Matthews tweaked his hamstring stretching a single into a double in the ninth inning. He came out before the home half of the ninth inning and was really never the same the rest of the season. The junior had eleven runs batted in and ten hits in the six games before the leg injury, temporarily solidifying the leadoff spot. It was the first time, but far from the last time, that Carolina would endure physical hardships. "I had a lot of confidence," Matthews said. "That kind of shot me back down. It hurt."

Vanquishing Florida on the road was not enough to do much to the chip the Gamecocks carried around with them, either. It will still present. It would be until late June, when they would again see the Gators. After the series win in Gainesville, Carolina went up just one spot, to third, in the *Baseball America* poll. It was still behind Vanderbilt and Virginia, teams it would face soon enough.

Chapter 5
Earning Respect

The Sunday win at Florida propelled South Carolina to a nine-game win streak, the longest of the regular season. Sweeps of SEC East opponents Kentucky and Tennessee were included in that run of victories, with Colby Holmes and Forrest Koumas taking off in their new roles as weekend starters. In their four combined outings against those two teams—and granted, the Wildcats and Volunteers were not the most productive offenses in the league—Holmes and Koumas pitched 25⅔ innings and gave up just three runs. They won three of the four decisions.

Koumas's April 3 start against Kentucky was particularly impressive, considering he had spent most of the week in the hospital. Koumas is highly allergic to peanuts, and he accidentally ingested pasta that had been cooked in peanut oil. The allergy caused Koumas to have difficulty breathing, which in turn made his ribs and back sore. "Visiting him in the hospital," pitching coach Jerry Meyers said, "I didn't think he was going to start that weekend."

He did, though. Koumas was discharged from the hospital Friday morning and on the Carolina Stadium mound Sunday afternoon. The coaches were surprised by that development, sure, but even more by what Koumas did in the game. He pitched into the seventh inning, giving up no runs on two hits.

Coach Ray Tanner credited Koumas's background as a high school quarterback in nearby Elgin for instilling that sort of toughness. "He took a lot of hits," Tanner said. "He wasn't a forty-five-passes-a-game kind of guy. He was running the ball. We liked that kind of toughness." The recovery, and subsequent outing, did not seem like it was all that big of a deal to Koumas. "I felt good before the game," he said after the victory. "I feel great now."

The Gamecocks lost two SEC series in 2010, to Florida and Kentucky. Those series were avenged in consecutive weeks in 2011, and Carolina, winners of 10 of 11, was on a roll. It had won 15 of 17 to run its record to 26-5, 10-2 in the SEC, by an April 12 trip to Charleston to face The Citadel.

The Bulldogs stunned the third-ranked Gamecocks, shutting them out 2–0 behind eight innings from left-hander Logan Cribb, who was making his first career start. It was only the second shutout of the Gamecocks since 2008. Third baseman Adrian Morales sat out, fearing he had a broken bone in his hand. It was announced at game time, too, that outfielder Jake Williams had been suspended indefinitely. Williams, twenty-one at the time, was charged with serving alcohol to minors at a house party. "I'm really disappointed," Tanner said then. "We didn't need that situation to arise."

One loss and one extenuating event had curbed the team's rhythm at an inopportune time. The Gamecocks were set days later to play the second number-one-ranked team in less than a month's time. Vanderbilt was coming to Carolina Stadium for three games.

The Friday night game against Vandy was another defining moment in Michael Roth's first full season as a starter. Blake Cooper, his predecessor as the Gamecocks' ace, had made a habit in 2010 of outdueling the other teams' best pitchers, even though he was operating at a disadvantage in terms of size and repertoire.

Roth was on a similar track in 2011. In the Kentucky series, he was up against right-hander Alex Meyer. Meyer went on to be the MLB draft's twenty-third overall pick.

Both pitchers went eight innings. Meyer was good. Roth was excellent. Meyer's line: three runs on six hits, five walks and eight strikeouts. Good. Roth's line: a run on three hits, a walk and six strikeouts. Excellent.

Like Cooper, Roth had learned how to elevate his game to another level when facing the more prototypical ace, by scouts' standards. He did it again to begin the Vanderbilt series, with right-hander Sonny Gray on the mound for the Commodores.

Gray was a savvy veteran who might have had the best pure stuff in the SEC. Despite being a hair under six feet tall, Gray could still deliver in the mid-nineties with his fastball, making his curveball and changeup very effective. Gray would eventually become the draft's eighteenth overall pick, property of the Oakland A's.

The results were strikingly similar to the Kentucky game—even down to the score, both 3–1 Carolina victories. Both starters went 7⅔ innings, but Roth again was better than a formidable foe.

Gray's line: three runs on eleven hits, a walk and seven strikeouts. Good. Roth's line: a run on three hits, two walks and eight strikeouts. Better. Note, too, that Vanderbilt's lineup—with Aaron Westlake and Jason Esposito anchoring it—was much, much better than that of Kentucky.

Offensively, all but one Carolina position starter, the ailing Morales, had a hit against Gray. Scott Wingo, Evan Marzilli and Adam Matthews—briefly back from his hamstring injury—each had two hits. Peter Mooney, batting in the leadoff spot, homered off Gray in the seventh inning.

At that point in the season, just past the halfway mark, Roth was 8-1 with a 1.24 earned run average. The left-handed specialist in 2010 had not allowed more than two earned runs in a game in nine starts to begin 2011. No one was all that surprised he was faring well—because of his laidback personality off the field and intensity on it—but *that* well? He was on his way to an All-America-type season. He had already shut down Clemson, Florida and Vanderbilt. "I knew he could pitch successfully," said David Roth, his dad, "but I must admit I never imagined he would develop into one of the country's top pitchers."

The heart of his pitching philosophy was strikingly simple. When he trotted it out for reporters late in the season, they laughed at the air of minimalism. His logic: it's harder to hit than pitch. He really believes that pitchers have the upper hand in every at-bat. In his mind, batters are the ones always trying to adjust to what the pitchers are doing. "It makes sense to me that it should be harder for a hitter to get a hit off me or score runs," he said. "That's just thinking logically about the game of baseball." Whether that's entirely true or not is irrelevant; it works for Roth.

There was an innocence to the way he approached the game, too. That was an ace up the ace's sleeve. Months later, Gray said on Twitter how much he enjoyed watching Roth pitch. His coach, discipline-oriented and old school as they come, admitted Roth had taught him to loosen up more than any player before him. "He had fun with it," Tanner said. "Watching Michael Roth play baseball is almost like, 'Okay, nobody in the stands and we're on a rec field.' It doesn't matter to him if you've got 8,500 people [watching] or you may be on national television. It's all the same to him."

Roth was evolving as the year progressed, too, using his intelligence—he is an international business major with a 3.8 grade-point average—to figure out tendencies and establish new wrinkles. Even for a veteran behind the plate such as Brady Thomas, Roth was a catcher's dream. "He's the easiest person I've ever caught in my life," Thomas said. "I could just set up my glove, call the pitch, close my eyes and know he was going to hit the mitt. I trusted him."

In one of his first starts, against Bakersfield, Roth was struggling to find his control early in the game. The umpire looked over toward the Carolina dugout at Meyers and Tanner. "This is your Friday night starter?" he said, raising an eyebrow. "Wow, I'm surprised."

Roth heard him. He wound up going eight innings that night to earn a victory. It was the first of eleven times in twenty starts that he would pitch into the eighth inning, or longer, in 2011. The joke was on the ump.

Pesky Vanderbilt leadoff hitter Tony Kemp went 5 for 5 in the second game, and Holmes was not nearly as sharp as he had been in his recent starts. Esposito and Mike Yastrzemski—yes, it's his grandson—homered off Holmes, who surrendered six earned runs in 4⅓ innings.

The Gamecocks, who scored three runs in the second inning, appeared as if they were up for a slugfest. But the deep and versatile Vandy bullpen slammed the door in Carolina's face. Five Commodores relievers combined to pitch the final three innings, giving up only one hit and striking out five. The 6–4 Vanderbilt victory set up another deciding Sunday game.

Meyers had no dilemma this time. It would be Koumas, who held the Commodores to one run in the first five innings. Vandy, though, broke a 1–1 tie in the sixth with back-to-back solo home runs by Westlake and Esposito, ending Koumas's day. The Gamecocks trailed by a pair of runs, but it seemed like 20 with the way the 'Dores relievers had pitched the previous day.

Carolina closer Matt Price was brought on in the seventh inning to try to keep Vanderbilt on 3 runs and give the hitters a chance in the final frames. Still down 3–1, the bottom of the seventh characterized a word South Carolina seized on as the season continued: battle. There was nothing pretty about what the Gamecocks did in that half-inning.

There were no majestic home runs, no moments of high drama. It was a steady stream of minor successes that turned into the biggest late-inning comeback of the year.

In an odd twist that week, pitcher Steven Neff was pressed into duty as a designated hitter, due to Williams's ongoing suspension and Matthews aggravating his hamstring the previous day. Neff grounded to first and flied to right in his first two at-bats—and then he led off the seventh with a double down the right-field line. Jaws dropped all over Carolina Stadium, including inside the home dugout. Neff had started taking batting practice on that Thursday, three days earlier, after more than a year of solely focusing on pitching. The Lancaster native was relying on unique athleticism and instincts. "We didn't expect him to do much," Roth said. "It was just one of those you've-got-to-be-kidding-me things. The pitching staff, in general, was just laughing and saying, 'This guy's an animal.'"

Something about that hit, which chased Vandy starter Taylor Hill, sparked Neff's teammates. South Carolina sent ten batters to the plate in the inning against the same bullpen that had dominated it on Saturday. The Gamecocks scored on a bases-loaded hit by pitch, a Jackie Bradley Jr. single to center field, a Wingo ground ball to the right side and a Thomas sacrifice fly.

It was 5–3 by the end of the four-run burst against the Commodores relievers. Neff, who actually took the loss as the starter at The Citadel, began and ended the inning at the plate. "It was almost laughable," Roth said. "Actually, it was laughable."

When it came to comedy, the most entertaining moment of the day was still to come. Price was in position for the win, if he could deliver the final six outs. Pitching with adrenaline after watching what his teammates had done, he blew the ball past Vandy in the eighth inning. Westlake struck out swinging, Esposito struck out looking and Yastrzemski struck out swinging. Price had overpowered Vanderbilt's 3-4-5 hitters, players who had all homered at least once during the weekend. Esposito had three home runs in the final two games.

One issue arose, though, for Price: because of a pinch hitter and runner in the eighth, the Gamecocks had done away with the designated hitter. Neff went to left field—and Price would have to hit in the bottom of the eighth. Price had always told teammates he was a big-time power hitter in American Legion ball, but it had been years since he had touched a bat. "I was scared going up there," he said months later. "I didn't know what to do. I was trying to remember what I did in high school."

The 2011 University of South Carolina Baseball Team's Run to Back-to-Back NCAA Championships

In an intense game and weekend, Price goofily standing in the batter's box provided levity. His teammates, coaches even, were cracking up. Some of that was happening in the press box and stands, too. As Price walked from the on-deck circle to the plate, the plan from Tanner was a simple one: put the bat on your shoulder, watch three strikes and then go pitch the ninth.

Tanner, though, called time in the middle of the at-bat. He walked out to talk with Price. He asked his All-America reliever, a guy with three wins and eleven saves at the time, if he could "punch it somewhere." Price, puzzled and still a bit fearful, said he would try.

Price then made contact, taking a weak hack that sent the ball back to the net behind him. The foul tip received loud applause from fans who were enjoying the awkwardness. Price then struck out on the 2-2 pitch, but he got a standing ovation from those in the seats. It was perhaps the most lauded strikeout by a home team's batter in college baseball history. "We were all on our toes watching," Roth said. "I think he closed his eyes and swung at that ball....He still talks about that at-bat."

Price still was able to do what comes most naturally. He finished off the Commodores in the ninth, earning his fourth victory. He struck out seven hitters in three innings. He at least made them meet the same fate he did.

For South Carolina, the 5–3 win was one of only four victories in 2011 when it trailed after six innings.

Another share-the-credit team victory had resulted in another epic series win, another takedown of a number-one team. Carolina would inch closer to the top spot, but it remained second, behind Virginia. The Gamecocks continued to harbor the anger over a lack of respect, though they would soon have a lot more issues than where they were ranked in the polls.

Chapter 6
Winning Anyway

South Carolina was 29-7 and ranked second in the country by the time it bussed to Mississippi State on April 21. The Gamecocks had taken series at Florida and against Vanderbilt, the SEC East teams that had started the year in front of them in the polls. They had won two of three against Clemson, too. It was close to an ideal start for the defending champs, excluding a midweek loss or two.

The season, though, threatened to crash down with one failed attempt at a diving catch.

Jackie Bradley Jr., an all-defensive-team center fielder, had made myriad outstanding catches for the Gamecocks since arriving in 2009, but something went dreadfully awry in the sixth inning of the Saturday game against the Bulldogs.

First baseman Ryan Collins sent a looping shot into right-center field, with Bradley playing straight away in center. The instinctive fielder initially thought he would get to the ball, as he so often did, but he eventually made a decision to dive. He slipped ever so slightly on grass still damp from overnight rains, and as he dove to make the catch, he landed awkwardly on his glove—and left wrist.

The collision with the ground jarred the ball free from his grasp, and Bradley jumped to retrieve it. In the rush of the moment, he didn't feel anything wrong with his left hand and wrist, no pain. But when he pointed his glove toward the infield, squaring himself to throw, he felt his wrist pop out of place. "I stopped," he said. "I even hesitated throwing. I ended up lobbing it in to Wingo."

Bradley reset his wrist in place and finished the half-inning, though television cameras were trained on Bradley flexing his wrist and looking at it. When he got back to the dugout, Ray Tanner asked if he was okay. Bradley said he thought he was. They were about to find out: Bradley was due up first in the top of the seventh.

Bradley picked up a bat to test it. As he started to swing, the weight of the bat again displaced his left wrist. "It was the worst pain I'd ever felt," he said. He was done for the day, but how long beyond that?

Bradley's prognosis would not be known until the team returned to Columbia, but there was still baseball remaining in Starkville. After a 5–3 loss to the Bulldogs on that Saturday, with Mississippi State taking the lead for good on the play in which Bradley was injured, it signaled the fourth Sunday rubber game of the Gamecocks' six SEC series to that point.

But who was left to play in the outfield? That was the thought even before sophomore Evan Marzilli had to go to the hospital late Saturday night with concerns about his heart. The team had lost two starting outfielders in a single day—and the other, Adam Matthews, was back on the shelf with the pesky hamstring issues.

Marzilli was in the intensive care unit for a bit before doctors decided the scare was not life-threatening. What Marzilli was experiencing, and had previously, was an intermittent rapid heartbeat. Tissue was blocking his heart from receiving a signal to regularly beat. In the coming days, he would need a procedure called an ablation to clear the blockage and allow the resumption of a normal heart rhythm. Like Bradley, his prognosis would not be known until the team got home. A mysterious news release was sent out by the school saying Marzilli had an undisclosed medical condition that was not a threat to his life.

Just before the season began, Bradley had joked that the Gamecocks' freakishly athletic outfield starters "could cover more ground than the world's oceans." By the end of April, Matthews had a leg problem, Bradley a wrist that wouldn't stay in place and Marzilli a heart beating erratically. "It got to a point where you'd look at yourself in the mirror and go, 'What else?'" Tanner said. "But what can you do? That's where the whole 'win anyway' thing got started."

Tanner had said that short phrase to his teams over the years, about the weather or injuries or variables of that nature. He would tell his players the circumstances did not matter; they had to find a way to win anyway.

The words took on new meaning in 2011, with everything swirling around. The message that day was roughly the same, but it had great urgency. Carolina was up against it.

"This is not going to be a situation where we're going to dwell on poor, pitiful us," Tanner told the Gamecocks before the Sunday game. "Let's go have some fun and do the best we can with what we've got and win anyway—find a way and have fun doing it."

Carolina had created a pattern of winning those rubber games in rewarding ways, but there was probably no more satisfying victory during the regular season—not Florida, nor Vanderbilt, nor any other—than the 13–4 tail-kicking of the Bulldogs. Steven Neff played left field, freshman DeSean Anderson played center and Jake Williams was the right fielder. And it was a good thing Williams was reinstated before the series began, after being cleared of any wrongdoing.

Neff struggled, going hitless in five at-bats, but Anderson and Williams combined to go 7 for 11. Three of their hits were doubles. Brady Thomas, batting cleanup, was 3 for 6 with four runs batted in. Christian Walker was 4 for 4 with a home run, his eighth of the year, and four runs batted in. The depleted lineup had thirteen runs and eighteen hits by game's end.

Koumas was ineffective—he lasted just 2⅔ innings—but he selected a good time for an off outing. His teammates, offensively and defensively, had come to the rescue. John Taylor pitched four innings to get the win, and Matt Price went the final 2⅓ innings to finish off the series.

"If I've ever had a special feeling with this team, it was the Sunday bus ride from Mississippi State," Chad Holbrook said. "That ride home was as gratifying of a feeling as you could have in the regular season."

Tanner was moved to see what his team had done. To win by nine runs under those conditions defied logic. Two of the team's outfielders probably needed some sort of surgery upon arrival in Columbia. It was one of the strangest weekends in recent memory, but it ended with two South Carolina victories. They had won anyway.

"We did it with guys who had been part-time players," Tanner said, pausing. "And we didn't miss a beat. To me, it was a magnifying moment. I told them, 'You guys, win, lose or draw, you're doing the best you can. You've answered the call, and I'm proud of you. The team concept, it's alive and well with this group. You have a chance.' We had a lot of baseball left, but we were in a good place."

Well, sort of.

Back in Columbia, doctors told Bradley that he had a slight tear in the triangular fibrous cartilage complex (TFCC) in his left wrist. It was causing his tendons to snap on and off the bone with each movement of the wrist. Bradley described the TFCC as an internal bracelet that holds the tendons to the bone.

It was not a good thing to tear, bottom line. He would need surgery; it was not optional. That would sideline him, he was told, for an estimated ten to twelve weeks. The College World Series started in about seven weeks. Those windows did not align.

Everyone thought Bradley's college career was over—everyone, that is, except the stubbornly determined Bradley. Bradley was all but a lock to be a first- or second-round pick in the June draft, even with a mediocre offensive season and the injury. The consensus was Bradley should just heal up for pro ball and not worry about playing again at Carolina. He had won a national title. He'd had a good run, but it was time to ride off into the million-dollar sunset.

"We thought that was it, yeah," Holbrook said. "We thought his career was over."

Bradley, though, was not hearing any of that. "I thought, 'Well, I don't know. If the team makes it far enough, I'm going to make a run at it,'" Bradley said. "'There's no way to stop me from playing.' That's the mindset I kept."

Bradley would return to Nashville for the surgery. He would again meet Dr. Douglas Weikert, a hand specialist at Vanderbilt's hospital, under unfortunate circumstances. Just before the 2010 season, the hamate bone in Bradley's right hand shattered when he was taking batting practice. Bradley made it back from that injury in about four weeks, ahead of schedule. That left him with some optimism that he might be able to return faster than the prognosis he was given for his wrist injury.

Meanwhile, South Carolina was preparing for life without Bradley. Tanner all but shrugged off Bradley's optimism. Even if Bradley was right, and he could return in Omaha, the Gamecocks would still have to find a way to get there without him. With Bradley pressing to impress scouts, his average had plummeted to .259. Regardless, the team would sorely miss his defense in center field.

There was a realistic feeling inside the coaches' locker room that the loss of Bradley could be prohibitive in terms of how far the Gamecocks could go in the postseason. "You don't know how long you can continue to keep going without being somewhat vulnerable," Tanner said.

Added Holbrook, "Thinking we were a national seed without Jackie wasn't part of our thought process. Sure, we told the players we weren't going to miss a beat, but we wondered behind closed doors if that would really be the case."

Even the coaches still had lessons to learn about their team. "Win anyway" had set in for the players the previous week at Mississippi State. There was no reason to doubt after that. The coaches would learn that, in time. "As it turns out, it brought the team—we were close already—but it made us closer," Holbrook said. "Adversity had a profound effect on our guys. They pulled together in an incredible way."

The Gamecocks wound up sweeping Auburn the following weekend. The first game, a 2–1 victory, was the tightest. With one out in the bottom of the ninth, they had the correct guy at the plate.

Scott Wingo stepped into the batter's box with Robert Beary, the potential winning run, standing on third base. Wingo had been terrible all night. He was 0 for 4, with three strikeouts in his past three at-bats. It took one swing, though, to reverse his fortune. He singled to center field, easily scoring Beary.

It was another Wingo walk-off. Night after night, game after game, it was as if all the magic from Omaha in 2010 had been spread through the entire 2011 season. The Gamecocks just kept winning, somehow and someway. Their coaches were wondering about them a bit, but the players did not share that viewpoint.

South Carolina was 35-8 and 17-4 in the SEC. "I don't think our future outlook wavered," pitcher Michael Roth said.

Chapter 7
Plugging Holes

After another SEC win, a 6–1 victory at Ole Miss on May 6, South Carolina appeared to be just about unstoppable. Sophomore Evan Marzilli's efforts that week supported the thought.

He had the procedure to correct his heart arrhythmia the Monday after the Auburn series. On Tuesday, Gamecocks coach Ray Tanner said Marzilli would be questionable for Wednesday's game at Wofford. Marzilli played, all right. He had three hits in three at-bats. "Impressive night by Evan Marzilli," assistant Chad Holbrook said that night on Twitter. "Heart ablation procedure on Monday and 3-for-3 performance on Wednesday. Tough kid."

Marzilli, one of the team's most valuable players in the 2010 postseason, then had two hits in the opener at Ole Miss. Robert Beary went 3 for 4 in the game. Beary was another story of resiliency and an illustration of the team concept Tanner talked about after the Mississippi State series.

By the end of the season, Beary had made starts at catcher, third base, left field, right field and designated hitter. That Friday in Oxford, he was in right field, where he settled in while the outfield dealt with the rash of injuries. Versatility had always been Beary's calling card, he said, and it was coming in rather handy for South Carolina. "It's something my mom taught me," Beary said. "She said, 'Learn them all. It makes you a more rounded athlete.' I was never scared to learn something new every day."

Pitcher-turned-position-player Steven Neff was in the lineup on a daily basis, either as an outfielder or designated hitter. The Gamecocks were doing their best to fill the gaps and compete. "It was a bunch of grinders," Holbrook said, "that's for sure."

That bunch of grinders ran into trouble that Saturday at Ole Miss when Colby Holmes and Tyler Webb were each hit for three early runs. The Gamecocks trailed 7–2 after six innings, and then the Rebels scored 3 more in the seventh to hand Carolina its worst loss of the season.

The team lost fourteen games in 2011 by a total of 42 runs, an average of 3 runs a loss. Take out the 8-run loss at Ole Miss, and the average loss shrinks to 2.6 runs a game. The Gamecocks were not used to losing games that were not at least competitive, within reach.

Still, true to the team's nature, they responded to contend on Sunday in the fifth SEC rubber game in eight conference series. The Gamecocks were finally on the wrong end of a close game, however. An Ole Miss error in the seventh led to a run to tie the game at 6, but the Rebels played small ball in the ninth to beat Matt Price and get a 7–6 walk-off series victory.

Those types of endings had all gone the Gamecocks' way until that point. It was South Carolina's first series loss. Was it an aberration or something to cause legitimate concern?

When the Gamecocks lost the opener against Arkansas the following Friday, some began to wonder if all the health issues were finally catching up with the team. Michael Roth had his worst outing of the year, giving up 3 runs on ten hits in 5⅓ innings in a 6–2 Hogs win in a game that did not start until 10:06 p.m. due to a lengthy rain delay.

Not only did Carolina lose the game, but it suffered another injury. Catcher Brady Thomas slipped as he was rounding first base after singling to begin the sixth inning. Going back to Bradley at Mississippi State, what was it about wet grass and sixth innings of losses that signaled bad news for the Gamecocks' health?

The outside of Thomas's left foot hit the bag awkwardly, and he said he "felt something strange in there." First base coach Sammy Esposito asked if Thomas was all right, and he said he wasn't sure. Beary's versatility again became very important. Thomas finished the game that night, but the captain caught just five of the team's final nineteen games. Between what turned out to be a stress fracture in his foot and a flare-up of the ulcerative colitis he had dealt with since he was a freshman at Florida State, Thomas was never really the same.

At the time of the injury, he was batting .335, third on the team behind steady first baseman Christian Walker and surprising second baseman Scott Wingo. Despite the bad foot, Thomas continued to embody the term "battle" that the team loved so much. He had three hits as a designated hitter the night after suffering the injury. His ability to turn on the ball was limited, but he served as the team's DH whenever he felt healthy enough to play.

For any game in which he played, Thomas said he received a pregame injection of Toradol. He wore a brace that made it impossible to fit his foot in his cleats, so he had to order new ones that he called "moon boots." He needed new soles for the shoes, too, so as to support the outside of the bone where the stress fracture was located. Just getting dressed for a game took an hour, at least.

Another team leader, Adrian Morales, had played through a minor break in his hand and chronically bad elbow tendinitis. While some Gamecocks, like Bradley, were obviously not healthy enough to play, the ones who could at all had to try. The team could not afford any additional sidelined veterans. Leaders such as Thomas and Morales had to show the way. And they did, through the pain.

As frustrating as it might have been, it was still a blessing Thomas was there at all. He had been granted an extra year by the NCAA just two weeks before the season began. Thomas's father, Tanner and the school's compliance office spent months going back and forth with the NCAA, trying to submit as much information as they could to support the idea that Thomas merited another year. "I wrote them my life story," he said.

Tanner felt strongly about the case, and it certainly seemed legitimate that Thomas had been through an ordeal upon arrival at Florida State. Due to his stomach being out of whack, he lost weight. He had no energy. He missed classes, workouts, practices. It affected his ability to function as a freshman, much less play baseball.

Years later, as Thomas awaited the NCAA's decision, the colitis again flared. It was often activated by stress, and it was a terribly tumultuous time for Thomas. What a sick twist. "It was eating me alive," he said. "My body was a mess, my health. I was almost as sick as I'd been with this condition."

Relief was on the way.

An application and appeal process that began in July 2010 ended on February 3, 2011, with Holbrook and pitching coach Jerry Meyers sitting in the dugout as Thomas headed out to run stadium stairs.

"You ready to practice?" Holbrook asked Thomas, wearing a straight face.

"What?" Thomas responded. "Are you kidding me?"

He was not. Thomas was on the field with his teammates that day, something he had longed for since the NCAA stopped letting him practice and work out with the team in the fall.

Tanner remembered seeing Thomas sitting alone in the stands one day when the team was practicing. His heart sank to see an isolated leader in limbo.

"It hit me. I thought, 'Boy, how much better we would be to have this guy with us,'" Tanner said. "I knew I wanted Brady in that dugout. I didn't know how much he'd play or what his role would be—how could you predict that?—but I knew I wanted him on that team. I knew that."

Even with a reduced role, due to the ailments, nothing could take that from Thomas and the Gamecocks.

Bill Wingo spotted Tanner at a high school awards banquet in 2007. Bill's son, Scott, would enroll at South Carolina later that year. Tanner was signing autographs in the front of a ballroom when Wingo found him. Dads are generally proud and biased when it comes to their kids. There was something different about this encounter, though.

"You've got something special when you've got Scott Wingo," Bill told Tanner, with Tanner's eyes widening. "I've coached him since he was four or five years old. He's a winner. He's a team player. Players like Scott, the guys like Scott."

Bill wasn't done. "He's going to help you get to the big dance one day," Bill said. "He's going to not only get you there but help you win one."

Bold words. But they were prophetic, considering who scored the run to win the 2010 College World Series.

Before Tanner got serious about recruiting Scott, he called Bill. Sort of like a boy who had just bought a ring, Tanner was calling to ask for the father's blessing. He wanted to run it by Bill since he had starred at Clemson in the early 1970s. It was a courteous move on Tanner's part, both toward the Wingos and Clemson. "If Scott's going to be a Tiger, I don't want to mess up the waters," Tanner told Bill, who said it would be okay with him to recruit Scott. Tanner continued. "Now," he said, "you know when you tell me I can do this that you have to realize he might be a Gamecock."

Wingo, from the Greenville suburb of Mauldin, visited Columbia soon after that conversation and committed not too long after that. Despite his thumbs up to Tanner, Bill admitted it still took time to get used to seeing Scott in "enemy" colors.

The transition from orange to garnet was cemented during a game at Clemson during Scott's freshman year. When Carolina shortstop Reese Havens was called out on a pickoff, Bill stood up and loudly jeered the umps. The Tigers fans around the Wingos, those who had known the Wingos for years, were floored. So that was how it was going to be, huh?

"I found out quickly that blood's pretty thick," Bill said with a laugh. "I surprised myself right then. It was kind of against tradition, my tradition. All of a sudden, you've got a kid out there playing for the other team."

In the retelling of the anecdote, Bill called Carolina "we."

Tanner was interested in Scott Wingo because of Bill Wingo—because of the family history in the game. If that sounds familiar, it's precisely why he went after former outfielder Whit Merrifield, the player who drove in Wingo to win the 2010 national title. He wanted Merrifield because of his father Bill's college success at Wake Forest. Same with Wingo. "I said, 'If I can get Billy Wingo's son, let's get him,'" Tanner said. "Hey, if you've got something like that to go on, you'd better pay attention."

Tanner confirmed that the banquet exchange did happen. "He kept telling me, a lot, 'You've got some good players, and he's going to help you,'" Tanner said. "'He's going to keep getting better.' I believed him. And he was right."

The .226 hitter his first three seasons at Carolina was at .331 on May 15, his bat working to go along with his plus defense at second base. He had won games against Georgia and Auburn with walk-off singles.

Against Arkansas, Wingo added another game-winning moment at another crucial time in another important SEC series. In game two, the Gamecocks took a 3–0 lead after two innings and were in control, up 5–1, after four. The Razorbacks, though, scored 2 in the sixth and 2 more in the eighth off a slumping Price to tie the game at 5.

The game remained tied heading to the bottom of the ninth, with Wingo due up first. How did that keep happening, Wingo batting in the ninth inning of tied SEC games at Carolina Stadium?

Wingo's older brother, Brad, was in the stands with a video camera. If you search for "Wingo Arkansas" on YouTube, it's the first video that pops up. There you'll find Brad, a former player at Spartanburg Methodist—as was their other brother, Gaston—narrating Scott's at-bat against Arkansas' Ryne Stanek.

"This guy was the ninety-ninth pick in the draft," Brad says before the 1-1 pitch. "Take him deep."

Then all you hear is screaming, the camera shaking wildly. Wingo had actually taken Stanek deep. The solo shot to right field was enough for a 6–5 Carolina victory.

This was a different Wingo, even from the national title season. This was the one Bill Wingo had promised Tanner, the improving player he could not do without. Scott had already been to the "big dance," as his dad had called it, but he was poised to get the team back to Omaha.

Riding the high from Wingo's latest walk-off, the Gamecocks had no problem with Arkansas in the sixth rubber game in nine SEC series. They won 7–1 on Sunday behind 8⅔ innings from Colby Holmes, who was nearly yanked from the rotation before the weekend. He was within an out of a shutout until Hogs right fielder Matt Vinson homered to end his day. But it was far from spoiled.

The offensive hero in the third game was…Neff. He again had the dugout in stitches, wondering how he was doing what he was doing. Neff, the guy who had not picked up a bat for a year until the previous month, homered in the fourth and eighth innings. Hitting in the 9 hole, Neff went 3 for 4 with three runs batted in. He went 6 for 8 in the series, with three home runs, a double and five runs batted in. Of Neff's eleven hits at the time, eight were for extra bases. Roth had it right when he called him an "animal."

Neff started—on the mound—two days later against UNC–Asheville, a 9–5 Carolina victory. With the unique variety of contributors, there was not another team in college baseball like this one. How far could it go?

First things first. The next three games would settle the SEC's regular-season championship.

Chapter 8

Standing Tall

The college baseball season began with most feeling as if Florida, South Carolina and Vanderbilt were the class of the Southeastern Conference—and the country, really. Entering the final weekend of conference play, that sentiment had been validated.

All three teams were in the top seven in the country, according to *Baseball America*. All three teams had 20-7 SEC records with three games to go. "To win 20 games, you think you've got a chance to win the thing," Gamecocks coach Ray Tanner said that week. "It ain't going to work this time. I'm surprised. It's amazing to me. You've got three teams at this point that have been able to get 20 wins with three to go."

With the earlier series wins against Florida and Vanderbilt, it at least held the head-to-head tiebreaker. But that would require a tie.

Florida (39-14) had the easiest draw, getting Kentucky (24-28) at home. South Carolina (42-11) had to travel to Alabama (31-22). Vanderbilt (42-8) had to go to Georgia (27-26), which had been playing well.

The Gamecocks were in a similar position in 2010, but Florida took two of three in Columbia to win the regular-season title. Even if it didn't work out again, Carolina had learned there were things beyond the conference race—much bigger things. "We're not putting our eggs into this one basket," game one starter Michael Roth said before the team left for Tuscaloosa, which had recently been ravaged by a tornado. "We want to win this weekend, but we want to win our last game again."

No matter how it shook out, *Baseball America* analyst Aaron Fitt projected all three East leaders to receive national seeds in the NCAA Tournament.

The top eight teams would earn the right to host both the regional and super regional rounds. The Gamecocks had hosted a regional the previous year, but Carolina Stadium had never held a super.

It would be a big start for Roth, individually. The lefty was 10-2 with a league-best 1.35 earned run average and eighty-three strikeouts in ninety-three innings. He was right in the middle of SEC Pitcher of the Year conversations.

Tanner and pitching coach Jerry Meyers had made him the Friday night starter. Roth made himself an ace. "What he's done, even if he doesn't do anything else, has been incredible," Tanner said then. "To have the numbers that he's had, I couldn't tell you I saw that coming. He's been really special. Not only has he been one of the best guys in the conference, but one of the best guys in the country. It's been great for us. It's been fun to watch."

Alabama's Nathan Kilcrease, though, was the better pitcher in the opener. Roth suffered his second loss in as many weeks, going over one hundred pitches by the sixth inning. Four walks hurt him. Still, he gave up just two runs (neither earned). The team was in it. Like Florida's Hudson Randall, Kilcrease was not going to break. He went the distance, giving up an unearned run on five hits and striking out five.

Florida was the only one of the three teams to win the weekend's first game, giving the Gators the advantage. But Kentucky had saved its top pitcher, future first-round pick Alex Meyer, for the second game. So there was still some hope. But the Gamecocks were probably going to have to find a way to win the series to win the league—and Roth had already taken his turn.

Peter Mooney, Scott Wingo and Evan Marzilli had three-hit nights in the second game in a 6–3 Carolina victory to even the series. Forrest Koumas, John Taylor and Matt Price gutted through to keep the Crimson Tide from getting too close. Price continued to be a bit hittable, though. In three innings, he gave up a pair of runs on five hits. The Gamecocks led 6–1, though, when he entered the game, so no damage was done. He earned his fourteenth save of the season in the victory.

Meyer and the Kentucky offense obliterated Florida 14–1 to allow Carolina and Vanderbilt back into the race. The Commodores had rebounded to win 9–3 in Athens. Nothing had changed entering the final day of the regular season: Carolina, Florida and Vanderbilt were all tied, then at 21-8.

This South Carolina season could only end this way. It would be the seventh of ten SEC series to come down to the final day. It would be the team's twelfth one-run game in fifty-six games. They were at that point a very strong 8-3 in those could-go-either-way games. That was something held over from 2010, really. In the super regional and College World Series, including the championship-sealing victory, the Gamecocks won four one-run games.

"If I were playing us, I'd be like, 'Gosh, these guys are good late,'" captain Brady Thomas said. "We were confident if we got in the late innings. We were confident the game was never over. The morale in the dugout would never be down. We'd keep fighting to the end."

If Carolina won, it would not matter what happened in Athens or Gainesville, since Florida and Vanderbilt had already lost a game in their respective series. The Gamecocks controlled their own fate.

A Christian Walker sacrifice fly gave Carolina a 1–0 lead after the first inning. Another Steven Neff home run, his fourth of the week, put the team up 2–0 after two. "Every time he got up to bat," Roth said, "everyone was taking bets on whether he was going to hit a home run." A Walker double to start the eighth, followed by an Adrian Morales single, made it a 3–1 lead. That bit of insurance from Morales, a player nicknamed Geico in 2010 because of his ability to pad late leads, would be key.

Alabama pushed across a run in the bottom of the eighth against John Taylor and Tyler Webb to cut the lead to 3–2. Cue Price. The closer had wobbled toward the end of the season, but he was sharp that day. He got the final four outs without giving up a hit, striking out two, for his fifteenth save of the season.

The Gamecocks' ninth one-run victory meant they had won the SEC championship, an accomplishment they had failed to achieve the previous year. The conference title under their belts, they moved up from third to first in the *Baseball America* poll. After the regular season, South Carolina ended where it felt as if it should have started.

No Jackie Bradley Jr., no Adam Matthews. Thomas and Morales were gimpy. But they had gone forty-four up and twelve down. It was going to be difficult to claim being an underdog in the postseason, but the Gamecocks would still try.

The bar at the SEC Tournament was set extremely low for South Carolina. Win a game—heck, score a couple of runs—and consider it a success, relative to the misery of the 2010 tourney.

The Gamecocks went 0-2 in suburban Birmingham in 2010, scoring a grand total of one run in twenty-one innings, including a twelve-inning loss to Auburn that sent the team home. With some extra time between the SEC and NCAA tourneys, Tanner held two-a-days that reminded the players of Little League, with a focus on fundamentals and basics. The team preferred to avoid a repeat of that.

Roth, for one, was determined. He was irked by dropping consecutive decisions to end the regular season, even if he had only given up two earned runs in those losses to Arkansas and Alabama. Tanner and Meyers had talked some that week with Roth. They were trying to figure out which day would be best for Roth to pitch to keep him on normal rest.

The junior looked at his coaches incredulously. To him, why was this even a question? He wanted the ball in the opener. He wanted the rotation kept intact. He wanted to be first. Tanner and Meyers shrugged. Roth had earned the right to decide that much. By choice, he would start against Auburn, and Koumas or Colby Holmes would go in the next game against either Georgia or Vanderbilt.

A Morales fielding error started the game against the Tigers—not what the Gamecocks wanted. Roth then gave up three hits that resulted in 3 unearned runs scoring. Carolina had not even batted yet, and it trailed 3–0.

Roth, though, did not yield another run. Something snapped into place after the first, and Roth became the pitcher who had started the season 10-1. He had been so-so in recent weeks, but he placed himself into gear against Auburn and remained there for the next month. Roth had 1-2-3 innings in five of the final eight frames. He retired the final thirteen Auburn hitters.

As for the offense, Morales's and Marzilli's run-scoring doubles in the second inning tied the game at 3. Marzilli went 2 for 2 against the Tigers, reaching base a total of four times. Going back to the second Alabama game, he had reached base eleven consecutive times, including nine hits. Marzilli bunted for a hit and later scored in the fourth. He was hit and scored in the sixth. His runs scored and driven in would have been enough to defeat Auburn 4–3. His teammates factored in, it was a 7–3 victory to erase the bad mojo from 2010 at Hoover Metropolitan Stadium.

The 2011 University of South Carolina Baseball Team's Run to Back-to-Back NCAA Championships

The good fortune did not last too long, however. With Sonny Gray on the mound the following day for Vanderbilt, the Gamecocks did not get much going offensively. Marzilli's streak ended with a second-inning strikeout. The Commodores were ranked fourth in the country, but they were somehow the four seed in the conference tournament—due to the fact the Western Division champ, Arkansas, had to automatically be the two seed.

The Gamecocks were running into Vandy too early, it seemed, and it was to their detriment. After a 7–2 loss, they fell to the losers' bracket. Once there, it was a dangerous proposition. Inherently deficient in pitching compared to Florida and Vandy, it would require the Gamecocks to really burn some arms if they wanted to get into the conference championship. Or they could catch their breath for the infinitely more important tournament that started the following week.

Carolina did not seem to have its typical gusto in an elimination game against Georgia, perhaps with an eye toward the NCAA Tourney. Even with a loss, just by defeating Auburn, it would still likely be a national seed. The Bulldogs scored 3 runs in the first inning, another in the second, and an early 4–2 cushion through three held up for the remainder of the game.

South Carolina was headed home after a 1-2 showing, but perhaps that was not the worst outcome for the Gamecocks. They had demonstrated a year earlier that they knew how to overcome Hoover heartbreak when June rolled around.

Chapter 9

Storming On

Carolina Stadium hosted its first NCAA Regional in 2010. Presuming the Gamecocks could get through the regional round in 2011, the home fans would see the program's first NCAA Super Regional at the four-year-old ballpark.

With a 45-14 record and the SEC regular-season championship on the shelf, South Carolina was the NCAA Tournament's number four overall seed. With the selection committee leaning heavily on the Ratings Percentage Index formula, the Gamecocks were behind Virginia, Florida and North Carolina. Vanderbilt was highly underrated as the six seed.

Incredibly, and without precedent, Carolina and Clemson were paired on the same side of the bracket. Like the Gamecocks, the Tigers would host a regional. The Palmetto State rivals were favored to play each other in a best-of-three super regional in Columbia. Before the tournament began, fans—and the teams—were trying to wrap their brains around that idea, given what had happened in Omaha in 2010 and during the regular-season series in March. If the sides were bitterly competitive—to the point of fighting—in March, what, then, would it be like with a trip to the College World Series on the line? It would be pure madness, Carolina Stadium awash in garnet, black and contempt.

"Some of the guys have looked ahead," South Carolina ace Michael Roth said after the draw was announced. "I'm sure you guys [reporters] would love it if we played them in a super regional. I'm not saying we wouldn't, too, but the media would have a field day. That's for sure."

The 2011 University of South Carolina Baseball Team's Run to Back-to-Back NCAA Championships

Gamecocks coach Ray Tanner politically said what he had to say, that his team was focused on the upcoming regional, not the potential matchup in the next round. "We realize we're matched up together," he said, "but I certainly think they've got a couple of teams to contend with up there and we've got a difficult field."

Tanner was posturing a bit. His team was decidedly better than the other three schools—Stetson, North Carolina State and Georgia Southern—in the Columbia regional. Clemson's regional test, though, was legitimately demanding. The second seed at Doug Kingsmore Stadium was Connecticut (41-17-1), and the third seed was in-state upstart Coastal Carolina (41-18), which had given Carolina all it wanted in the 2010 super regional in Myrtle Beach.

Still, the Tigers won their first two games, defeating Sacred Heart 11–1 and Coastal 12–7, to reach the regional final. Connecticut or Coastal would have to win three games in two days, including twice against the home team, to pull the upset. It had been done before, but not very often.

With the Gamecocks opening their regional against Georgia Southern, much of the talk that week centered on prolific Eagles outfielder Victor Roache. The sophomore had thirty home runs, eight more at the time than anyone in the country, and eighty-three runs batted in. So much for the new bats holding back power and production. "He didn't hit one in that last game," Tanner said, half-jokingly, "so I'm a little worried."

Roache, though, had not seen Roth, or any pitcher of that caliber, in the Southern Conference. He flied out to center against Roth in the first, walked in a scoreless fourth and grounded out to third in the seventh. It was fitting that he came up in the ninth inning, with his team down a run, to face Carolina closer Matt Price. Price versus Roache was power on power. Heart rates increased at Carolina Stadium until Price got Roache to strike out looking to end the game. The 2–1 Gamecocks victory was their tenth one-run win of the season. It was Price's NCAA-leading sixteenth save. Roth moved to 12-3.

South Carolina scored in the fourth on a Brady Thomas sacrifice fly and in the sixth on an Adrian Morales single to right that scored Christian Walker. It was Thomas's last time catching for the Gamecocks. He had aggravated the stress fracture in his left foot during the SEC Tournament, and after giving it a go against Georgia Southern, he was relegated to be the team's designated hitter.

That opened the door for Robert Beary to get more comfortable behind the plate. He had been a work in progress at the demanding position, since he was divided between so many spots on the field. But he had caught five of the previous nine games, establishing himself there to some extent. That would prove important during the course of the month, including in the regional.

Trailing 1–0 early the next day against Stetson, Carolina exploded for 6 runs in the third inning, 4 of the runs scored on a grand slam into the left-field seats by Beary, the eventual regional MVP. With 4 more runs in the next inning, the Gamecocks went on to rout the Hatters 11–5 to advance to the regional final.

Stetson knocked out North Carolina State, keeping Tanner from a meeting with his alma mater, to get a rematch with the Gamecocks. The game took two days to complete, due to a severe thunderstorm that rolled through the stadium area during the fifth inning on that Sunday night. The winds, gusting to sixty miles an hour, ripped the tarp covering the field and moved large tractors that were meant to anchor the tarp. The storm took large panels of aluminum siding from adjacent buildings and threw them on the ballpark's grounds.

No one was hurt, even though some fans had to huddle in bathrooms and under nearby bridges to avoid the severe conditions. Others sat in their cars, the wind jostling them. The game could not be resumed that night because a medium-sized tree had fallen across power lines, blowing out a transformer beyond the left-center-field wall. No electricity, no baseball.

Crews from South Carolina Electric & Gas restored power to the stadium around 1:30 a.m. Monday morning. That left stadium workers and volunteers about twelve hours to get the place ready for a 1:00 p.m. resumption. "Everybody knew what we had to do," said Jeff Davis, the school's athletics facilities director. "Our goal was to get it ready as if nothing happened. Everybody just pitched in to make it happen."

Stadium in good shape and the regional resumed, South Carolina's goal was to prevent another game—a deciding game with the Hatters—from being played that night. The Gamecocks led 5–1 at the time of the delay, and they did not want to have momentum go sliding in the other direction because of the strange circumstances.

It started to shift toward Stetson a bit in the eighth inning. The bases were loaded with one out when Price was summoned to get the final five outs.

One run scored, on a throwing error by Morales, but Price got the team out of the inning with a 5–2 lead. Four Gamecocks runs in the top of the ninth created some breathing room, and Price got a strikeout and double play to seal an 8–2 victory.

The Gamecocks had advanced to their second super regional in as many years, and it would be their first at Carolina Stadium. But who would they play?

Connecticut defeated Coastal 12–6 in the Sunday elimination game, meaning the Huskies and Tigers would see each other that evening for the first time in the regional. The teams went back and forth all night. Clemson went ahead 4–1 after five and a half innings, but UConn came back with two runs to chop the deficit to 4–3 through six. It then scored three in the bottom of the eighth to lead 6–4 entering the ninth.

Trying to avoid a winner-take-all game the following night, the Tigers came up with the tying runs in their final at-bats. A Spencer Kieboom two-out, two-run single evened the score at six entering the bottom of the inning.

Connecticut, however, just kept coming. The heart of the Huskies order got to Clemson closer Scott Weismann, and Ryan Fuller's two-out single scored former Major Leaguer Lee Mazzilli's son L.J. with the winning run.

The Tigers might as well have stopped playing right then, ceding the regional to UConn. The Huskies blistered Clemson in the Monday final, scoring 3 runs in the first, 5 more in the fifth and 6 in the eighth for a 14–1 throttling to end the hopes of a Carolina-Clemson super regional.

With three victories in two days in a foreign stadium, UConn would be the Gamecocks' opponent in the best-of-three. The winner was going to Omaha.

Connecticut's comeback at Clemson was impressive. So was its star power. Northern teams are typically clamoring for acceptance and respect, because the game lies in virtual obscurity there, but there was little to doubt about the Huskies by the time they arrived in Columbia.

Earlier in the week, UConn center fielder George Springer was the eleventh overall pick in the MLB draft. He came into the series with a .350 average, 12 home runs, 77 RBIs and 31 stolen bases. And hitting was not even his best attribute. The only center fielder in the country on his level defensively was Jackie Bradley Jr., the Carolina star still out with the wrist injury. The pair had played together the previous summer on Team USA's collegiate team.

The team's ace, Matt Barnes, went eight picks after Springer. Barnes came in 11-4 with a 1.62 ERA. Bradley and Barnes were both selected by the Red Sox.

UConn was playing its Monday game against Clemson when both players were selected. Springer was informed literally on his way to the plate. "That was something pretty weird," he said.

Beyond its talent, the Huskies also seemed to embody the Gamecocks' light-and-loose approach to the game. They played laser tag the night before the series began. Before their pressure-packed regional final at Clemson, they were doing backflips in the outfield and playing Wiffle Ball.

UConn was not to be taken as a speed bump, and Carolina was well aware. Still, the Gamecocks were playing at home, where they were 34-4 and had won all of their three-game series in 2011.

Game one pitted Barnes and Roth, who was selected the preceding Monday in the thirty-first round—compared to Barnes in the first. It placed the Carolina left-hander in familiar territory, tangling with a pitcher that had scouts oohing and aahing. It did not affect Roth, really, other than to boost him in the same way it did the team when it was not ranked number one. "He doesn't throw 97," Tanner said. "He's not going to dominate you with that. But he's going to dominate you with what he's got."

Just as he had against Kentucky's Alex Meyer and Vanderbilt's Sonny Gray, first-rounders like Barnes, Roth slayed a giant. The junior went 8⅓ innings, giving up an unearned run on six hits, with three walks and two strikeouts. John Taylor, making his forty-fourth appearance of the season, got the final two outs in Carolina's 5–1 victory.

Barnes retired eight of the first nine batters, striking out four, but he was vulnerable the second and third times through the order. Neff had two more hits, including another double. Barnes exited in the fifth, having allowed five earned runs on eight hits. The offense had helped Roth, though he needed little assistance.

In his three postseason starts in 2011, Roth was 3-0 and had not given up a run in 24⅓ innings. For the year, he was 13-3 with a 1.02 earned-run average. "We found out why Michael Roth is one of the best pitchers in the country," UConn coach Jim Penders said. "I thought the team that played better won the ballgame."

The 2011 University of South Carolina Baseball Team's Run to Back-to-Back NCAA Championships

South Carolina, the defending national champ, was a single win away from returning to the College World Series. Its longest losing streak of the season was two games and that had happened just twice, both away from Carolina Stadium. The Gamecocks could almost smell and taste the whiskey filets at the Drover steakhouse and feel the Omaha grass beneath their feet.

On a night in which the team could clinch, the Gamecocks and Huskies were tied 2–2 entering the eighth inning. It had to be another close game, right?

The position was eerily familiar for Walker, who would lead off the inning. His three-run home run in the eighth inning of the 2010 super regional in Myrtle Beach effectively sent Carolina back to Omaha for the first time in six years.

The Gamecocks did not need three runs in 2011. Walker's solo homer off tiring UConn starter Greg Nappo sufficed to do the same thing. The home team led 3–2, and Price was on the mound. Sensing the imminent, the sold-out crowd of 8,242 inside Carolina Stadium was frenzied.

Price pitched around a hit in a scoreless eighth inning, and then, suddenly, UConn's bullpen could not get an out in the ninth. A five-run frame for South Carolina stretched the lead to 8–2. With Price on the mound, the Huskies were done.

Price struck out the final two batters, earning his eighteenth save. The fans exploded as the Gamecocks dog piled in front of the mound. It was the first time since 2004 that they had seen in person their team celebrate a trip to college baseball's Promised Land.

South Carolina was again in the College World Series, making the program's tenth appearance since 1975. The Gamecocks, in position to defend their 2010 title, were 50-14. "That's truly amazing," Tanner said. "And we'll get a chance to play some more."

Chapter 10
Gaining Perspective

Omaha had fallen for the Gamecocks during their 2010 run to the national championship. They were taken with the scrappy bunch with infectious personalities such as Jackie Bradley Jr., Michael Roth and Scott Wingo. So there was some excitement in Nebraska's largest city to know that South Carolina, the champs, would be back. For one thing, it allowed for some continuity with the College World Series, now that $131 million TD Ameritrade Park was the new site and Rosenblatt Stadium had closed its doors after six decades of hosting the summer spectacle.

The Gamecocks' super regional win was not celebrated anywhere more enthusiastically than a century-old two-story home on Thirty-third Street in south Omaha. Inside, the Peters family erupted when Robert Beary squeezed the final strike. The joy spilled into the typically quiet neighborhood street. "It was like ten o'clock," said Charlie Peters, thirteen years old, who was joined by his younger brother Max. They weren't wearing shirts or shoes, but Charlie was wearing a Carolina cap. "We ran down the street, waving stuff in the air and screaming. We were out there doing that for like ten minutes."

Why the fuss? Why would a team that plays its games 1,200 miles away be of that much interest to those kids, as well as their parents? Neither Jenny nor Matt Peters went to South Carolina. The family had barely even passed through the state.

But the Peterses developed a soft spot for the Gamecocks long before, in 2003. Playing in Omaha that summer, South Carolina's coaches and players walked through the doors at Children's Hospital and Medical Center. The team had an off day in the series, and it wanted to spend time encouraging the young patients and their families.

Charlie, then five, was lying in a hospital bed. He was weak, but he perked up a bit when he saw the ballplayers. He told them he wanted to be like them one day. They even got Charlie up to play a game of "air baseball" in the lobby. There was a bat but no ball, and the rules were made up along the way. "Step on me," a player would say, "I'm a base."

"They were so animated," said Jenny, the energetic mother of, at that time, six kids. They were also different. Every team in the College World Series came through the hospital in 2003; one stuck out. "They were the ones who were the real deal," Jenny said. "They wanted to know Charlie as a friend. That was the coolest part of the whole thing."

One player asked to hold Charlie's sister Emma, who was about six months old at the time. The Gamecocks also asked lots of questions. What was wrong with Charlie? Would he get better? Could he come watch them play?

Two months removed from a harrowing diagnosis, but one all too familiar to the family, Jenny and Matt Peters had some of those same questions.

Charlie moped around the house the last full week of April 2003. He looked and felt worse with each passing day, so much that Matt, his dad, almost skipped a business trip to Connecticut to stay with him. But Jenny urged Matt to go anyway.

On the twenty-ninth of that month, a Tuesday, Jenny called Matt from the doctor's office. Charlie had been throwing up so much that she decided it was time to see what was going on. What she learned there changed the family's trajectory. She had to call Matt back later in the day. "It's cancer," Jenny told Matt.

Charlie had Burkitt's lymphoma, a form of the disease that often affects children. A tumor in his chest was doubling in size every twenty-four hours.

The family's pediatrician, Joe Straley, was sitting with Jenny when the radiologist called to report the bad news. "She was very cool, very matter of fact," Straley remembered. "She said, 'Well, let's get after it.' They emotionally were able to get over that terror and denial and fear and moved on to acceptance and taking care of it."

A reason for that reaction was that this was territory already traveled for the Peterses. They had been down this road with their firstborn, Morgan. Five years before Charlie's diagnosis, Jenny and Matt learned that Morgan had another form of childhood cancer called rhabdomyosarcoma. As it sets in, it begins to eat at the bones. By the time it was discovered in Morgan's cheek, it had already damaged her hearing. If the family had not acted when it did, her survival rate would have plummeted.

As it was, Morgan was able to beat the disease after surgery and rest. By 2011, she was twenty years old and in college at Missouri Western. She planned to be a nurse to help others through their medical trials. She still could only hear out of one ear, but the impairment had not halted her drive. "It's so typical of these wonderful kids," Jenny said. "They want to give back."

Matt and Jenny were not even thirty years old when they had their first encounter with cancer, and round two was coming. Charlie was twelve days old when Morgan got sick. Five years later, something similar was happening to him. "I couldn't believe it," Matt said. "I remember thinking, 'I cannot believe we're doing this again.'"

Jenny might have seemed "cool" to the doctor on the outside, but her emotions were churning. "You have to think, 'What are the odds we're going to make it again?'" she said. "You have this crushing, sinking feeling. You have a hope your faith will see you through it. We never asked why, because we knew God would see us through it."

Matt hustled back from New England, and the couple learned that the ensuing two days would be critical to Charlie's chances of survival. "We almost have to kill your child to save him," the oncologists told Jenny and Matt. "If he can make it through the next forty-eight hours, we have a shot."

Just two hours from the end of that critical window, Charlie's monitors began sounding off. His heartbeat was beating rapidly, wildly. He was rushed in for additional surgery.

Jenny and Matt hit their knees, praying in front of a candle that said "Let the Children Come to Me." They looked to the sky and asked, "Now what?"

"Cancer does that," Matt said. "We were humbled. You have no choice. It brings you to the ground, to your knees."

Relieved, the surgeons told the parents that it was a false alarm. The catheter had been pushed in too far against Charlie's heart, which was causing it to beat erratically. A slight adjustment and Charlie made it through the forty-eight-hour window. His body had begun to fight. He had highs and lows in the coming weeks, but he was generally improving.

He wasn't having the best day when the Gamecocks arrived in June, but their appearance helped. "He was so weak he could hardly move around to play with us," said Wade Jordan, a pitcher on the 2003 team. "Seeing how he lit up with all the guys there, it was an amazing thing to see."

He really came alive when Tanner asked Charlie and his parents if they would like to come to one of Carolina's College World Series games. He wanted Charlie to be an honorary batboy.

Charlie spent time alternating between the dugout and Jenny's lap during the Gamecocks' 11–10 victory that knocked out second-seeded Louisiana State. He did not have enough energy to stay down with the team, but he tried whenever he could. "He could barely keep that helmet on his head," Jenny said. "He gave it all he could running out there to get those bats. He felt like such a hero."

Years later, Tanner still recalled a snapshot in his mind of Charlie leaning against the wall of the dugout. "I can still see his face today," Tanner said. "It's one of those things that sticks with you. He was fighting for his life, but there was joy. There was some happiness that was reaching out to be a part of what we were doing at the time. I can still remember thinking, 'Wow.'"

In that moment, Tanner decided he wanted this, the friendship with Charlie, to be more than a hospital visit and the 2003 College World Series. He wanted it to extend. He wanted to help. It was fairly characteristic of Tanner, considering he had started a foundation—along with his wife, Karen—to help children who were sick and in need.

Tanner had instilled some of those humanitarian qualities in his players, as well. Jordan said he was so shy then that he was afraid to talk to waitresses, but he mustered the courage to ask Jenny for the family's home phone number so he could keep up with Charlie's progress. Sure enough, Jordan called every month or two to check on Charlie.

"When you look back at it, nobody really remembers what we did on the field," said Jordan, twenty-eight years old and living in New Zion, South Carolina, in 2011. "But they remember that kid. All we did was take a little bit of our time to create something that was bigger than baseball."

Straley, the pediatrician, said he has seen a lot of athletic teams visit sick kids. But not like South Carolina. "Teams come up and they swing through and they make a huge impact and the kids make an impact on the team," he said, "but then they're on to the rest of their lives. That wasn't the case with Charlie and the Gamecocks."

About a week after the team left, Charlie's health reversed course. A fungal infection had taken hold where the surgical scar was left on his chest. "Things went from bad to rotten really fast," Jenny said. Without a functioning immune system, the infection was devouring his chest at an alarming rate.

Charlie had all but beaten the cancer by that time, but the fungus, known as aspergillosis, offered much worse odds because Charlie's body had no way to stop it. At one point, the doctors leveled with the Peterses. They couldn't even look the couple in the eye as they said Charlie had less than a 10 percent chance of living. It was somewhere around 7 percent, compared to the 70 percent success rate with the lymphoma.

"We'd kind of hit rock bottom at that point," Jenny said. "We're going, 'Come on, this poor kid is trying so hard.'"

Charlie had surgery and then started a brutal cycle of medication nicknamed "Antiterrible" because of its side effects in ridding the body of the fungus. "We almost lost him a few times that summer," Jenny said, wincing as she produced those words.

Rough as it might have been, the medicine worked. Doctors had difficulty explaining why or how, but Charlie began to improve toward the end of the summer. By August, he was just another kid in the large family. There was no way to pick him—or Morgan, for that matter—out of the lineup as the cancer survivor. "That's when we felt like we got our son back," Jenny said.

Soon after, Charlie wanted to send a gift to South Carolina's baseball team to thank it for the support and friendship. He mailed a bucket of sunflower seeds and bubble gum to the team. He included a poster, too. Jenny asked Charlie what he wanted the message to say. "I would tell them never to give up," he told his mom. Sounded good to her. They pasted on it a picture of Charlie sitting in the dugout and wrote "Never Give Up!" above it. A month or so later, the Peterses got something back from South Carolina. A note from Tanner included a picture of the poster's resting place in the training room. Charlie was inspiring the Gamecocks, even from afar.

South Carolina, as fate had it, again played in the College World Series in 2004. By then, Charlie was healthy. "To see him recovered," Karen Tanner said, "it meant more than I could ever describe."

The 2011 University of South Carolina Baseball Team's Run to Back-to-Back NCAA Championships

You would think a six-year absence in Omaha would be enough to sever the relationship. By the time the Gamecocks were again in the College World Series, in 2010, the players had obviously left, and so had some of the team's coaches. But Tanner was still there, even if he needed a reminder to call Charlie.

It had been in the back of his mind until the Gamecocks lost their opener to Oklahoma. Then Tanner knew the team needed Charlie—he needed Charlie. The family was invited to the next game against Arizona State.

Charlie, then twelve, brought with him another poster. It had a picture of him in his hospital bed in 2003, weak and his future bleak, and then a picture of him in 2010, healthy and his future bright. He had even started playing baseball. He sometimes played in the outfield, others at second base. He pitched some, too. Charlie had been good to his promise to the 2003 Gamecocks that he would one day be like them. Tanner has joked that he's leaving a scholarship open for him.

With Charlie at Rosenblatt, the Gamecocks did not lose again. They played inspired by the memory of seven-year-old Bayler Teal, who lost his battle with cancer during the College World Series. And they were motivated by Charlie's presence, which provided perspective about the division between the game of baseball and the game of life.

"I see his face all the time," Tanner said. "I envision him on the rail of the dugout. It's amazing. Yeah, I'm the old coach, but you have experiences in your life that grab and influence you. Certainly Charlie Peters and Bayler, how they were involved in our program and lives, that's really, really big and special."

The team won an event-record six consecutive games in 2010 to claim the school's first meaningful national championship.

Who do you think got the first call when South Carolina got back in 2011? That's right; it was the kid running up and down the street celebrating their return.

Tanner asked Charlie if he would like to be the team's official batboy for the tournament. He was going to have to miss a Little League game or two. But it seemed like a good excuse.

"I was really happy," he said. "I'm glad we stayed in touch like this."

Chapter 11
Mending Quickly

One of Charlie Peters's favorite South Carolina players was center fielder Jackie Bradley Jr., the 2010 College World Series' Most Outstanding Player. The Gamecocks were returning to Omaha, but would Peters get to see Bradley play there in 2011?

Bradley tore wrist cartilage on April 23 and had surgery six days later to repair it. The consensus was that the junior, the fortieth overall pick in the MLB draft, had played his last college game. Bradley, though, had not resigned himself to that fate. He remained determined that he would play again if the team advanced to the College World Series. "He kept imploring his teammates," lead assistant Chad Holbrook said, "'Keep winning, keep winning, and I might be able to play again.'"

It still sounded like a fantasy to many, but that changed in the days before the team left for Omaha. On June 14, two days before the team was scheduled to depart from Columbia, Bradley was given clearance by doctors to again start hitting. He swung the bat on that Tuesday to demonstrate to the coaches and trainers that he was in no pain. There was hope. "It's still a long way to go," Tanner said, "but it's only Tuesday."

The Gamecocks' College World Series opener was the following Sunday evening against Texas A&M. Was it realistic to think that Bradley could make enough progress in five days to actually play? "Could you see him in a game, possibly? Yes," Tanner said. "In a starting situation? Probably not." But then again, Tanner had not expected Bradley to even get back to this point—not this fast, anyway. Bradley was given a ten- to twelve-week prognosis, and he was just past the eighth week. His reputation as a quick healer had again been affirmed.

The following day, Bradley hit off a tee. That was the second of the baby steps toward playing. He felt no pain. He would participate that Thursday in batting practice in Omaha. If that went well, there was no reason to believe that Tanner would not at least put him on the Gamecocks' twenty-seven-man roster for the College World Series. As Tanner had said, Bradley could at the very least provide late defensive help in center field. Knowing Bradley, there was no reason to count him out of anything shy of again being the event's MVP.

"It's not like we're going to get any worse with him coming back," first baseman Christian Walker said.

Coaches, teammates and media members gathered around the cage at a west Omaha field to see how Bradley's batting practice session would go. "I was hoping I didn't swing and miss at the first pitch," Bradley said. It took him a little while to get warmed up, but by his final turn, the left-handed-hitting Bradley was shooting line drives into right-center field. More importantly, he experienced no pain in his left wrist. "I thought he looked great, actually," Tanner said. "He wasn't tentative. He looked healthy."

Tanner's stubborn, resilient All-American had left him no choice. Of course he had to include Bradley on the roster. "I think we're going to have to put him on there," Tanner said. "He looks good to me."

It was essentially a miracle that Bradley, who had quietly watched the regional and super regional from the stands, was ready to play. He backed up what he had been telling his teammates. "Make it to Omaha," he would say, "and I'll be back."

Bradley was healthy, but another roadblock remained: his average had been all the way down to .259 before the wrist injury. It was not as if he had exactly been knocking the cover off the ball when he was physically fine. Now he was going to come back just in time to see the best pitching in the country. How would that work?

The coaches were not as concerned as you might suspect. They felt as if Bradley had been pressing to impress Major League scouts. Now that he had already been selected by the Boston Red Sox, they thought he might be more relaxed. Plus, even if he was off at the plate, he still added a lot of value in the field.

Bradley was so dedicated to keeping his defensive instincts sharp that he had taken fielding practice each day with his teammates, putting a glove on his off hand, his right hand. He had planned all along to play again with the Gamecocks, whether anyone chose to believe him or not.

Tanner's drive-by of the TD Ameritrade Park construction site the previous summer had proven prophetic. South Carolina was back, armed with the claim of closing down Rosenblatt and opening up the new ballpark.

The old stadium looked lonely in south Omaha, just off Interstate 80. The only reason it was still standing by June 2011 was because the neighboring zoo had not raised enough money to raze it. An auction—in which seats and other pieces of the stadium were sold—took place during the College World Series. Late on the Saturday afternoon before the championship series, a crew of city workers took down the Rosenblatt Stadium sign.

Some Omahans had gotten over the change. They were ready to embrace the future at the $131 million stadium, which was much closer to downtown and its attractions. Others, though, felt as if they could never transition from the neighborhood that had become so friendly, so familiar, to a corporate bonanza. Omaha was the battlefield of an emotional tug-of-war as the series approached.

"We're obviously sorry to see Rosenblatt go," said Steve Rosenblatt, the son of former Omaha mayor and stadium namesake Johnny Rosenblatt, "but when fans get here and see the new facility, they're going to fall in love. We'll never get over missing Rosenblatt, but we've got to understand that time moves on. They've created a great facility; we've got to embrace it."

As is the case with most new stadiums on the Major League and Minor League levels, TD Ameritrade was primarily constructed to increase revenue through private suites. Rosenblatt had some stationed down the first-base line, but officials and designers wanted to give the high rollers a better vantage point, behind the plate, at TD Ameritrade. Sight lines were improved for everyone. So were the dugouts and locker rooms.

Capacity would remain the same, close to twenty-five thousand, but TD Ameritrade allowed fans to walk all the way around the stadium. At Rosenblatt, the outfield seats were cut off from the main concourse, which was like a dungeon under the stands. At the new facility, the concourse was above the lower level, so if you were inclined, you could hang out behind the sections and still see the game.

Some things, though, simply could not be improved or upgraded. The new stadium was situated in the middle of an up-and-coming entertainment district called NoDo, short for North Downtown. The old stadium was in the heart of a middle-class neighborhood with far more houses than bars. The famous Zesto, with its burgers and milkshakes, was a block away. Greg Pivovar's Stadium View Cards, a sports memorabilia shop that handed out free beers during the tournament, was across Thirteenth Street.

Charm is something that takes decades and decades to develop. That will take time at TD Ameritrade Park. "We're starting all over again," said Pivovar, an attorney who opened the store twenty years earlier as a hobby. "It's different."

Tanner and others theorized that baseball—real, live baseball—might bring around some of those slow to adapt. It arrived on June 18, a beautiful Saturday afternoon in Omaha. Former president George W. Bush, a baseball fanatic and former part owner of the Texas Rangers, delivered the ceremonial first pitch. North Carolina and Vanderbilt, the third and sixth seeds, began tournament play with a 7–3 Commodores victory.

It was the first time that three teams from the same division—the SEC East's Carolina, Florida and Vandy—had reached the College World Series. But only one was the returning champion. There were Gamecocks T-shirts everywhere in the streets around the stadium, and most wearing them were Nebraskans who remembered the adventure in 2010.

One of the team's stars was literally the poster boy for the series. Michael Roth was on College World Series billboards all across the city, including one affixed to the side of the stadium. You'd better believe his teammates had a good time with that. "They asked me if my head would fit to get in and out of the bus," Roth said. "It was kind of weird seeing yourself everywhere. I thought they might use the dog pile or something like that. It was kind of cool, I guess. My family enjoyed it."

At the opening ceremonies on Friday night, Roth was honored as the Elite 88 award winner. The Elite 88 goes to the top academic player in each of the NCAA's eighty-eight championship sports. "Yeah, I was officially the biggest nerd at the College World Series," said Roth, who had a 3.82 grade-point average in international business. Roth would make a case that he was also one of the best players at the College World Series.

It was time for South Carolina's title defense. It wanted to return to Omaha, and it was there.

The lineup for the Sunday opener against Texas A&M was handed out in the press box about an hour before the game. The very thing Tanner called improbable the previous week had become reality: Jackie Bradley Jr. was in the starting lineup, batting second.

The lineup was shuffled a few minutes later, after Evan Marzilli's hamstring—tweaked a few days earlier—was deemed healthy enough for the sophomore to play. That bumped Bradley down to ninth, which would effectively take some pressure off him. Still, Bradley was playing—and starting—to begin the College World Series. Those who had doubted him—and there were many—had learned a lesson. "He wanted to get out there again," Holbrook said. "He didn't want the Mississippi State game to be his last game in college."

Bradley's return was a charge for a team that was already playing well. The Gamecocks and Florida were the only two teams in the College World Series that had not lost an NCAA Tournament game.

About the only people left chagrined about Bradley were those involved with the Boston Red Sox. They feared he was returning too quickly and risking additional injury to his wrist. That's a natural feeling to have about an early round draft pick. Bradley just shrugged off their concerns; playing with Carolina was his priority. "I wasn't with Boston then," he said. "By me being on the field, that's what was going to give us the best chance of winning. I was good enough to play. That's how I felt. That's how I feel now, to this day."

With Bradley again in tow, perhaps 2011 was finally the year to exorcise the team's curse of the Omaha opener. In a game that took eight and a half hours due to multiple lightning delays, Carolina lost to Oklahoma in its first game in 2010—and then reeled off a College World Series–record six victories, including four in elimination games, to capture the title the hard way.

The Gamecocks had lost seven consecutive Omaha openers, going back to 1977. Before 2010, they had not even scored in one since 1982. Tanner himself was 0-4 in College World Series openers.

So when Texas A&M scored four runs in the top of the first against Roth and South Carolina, you would think a sense of panic—and familiarity—might have set in. That was not the case, however—not with these Gamecocks. They had been through enough to know the past did not dictate their present or future conditions. The team had even played a similar game in the SEC Tournament, trailing Auburn by 3 after the top of the first. It won 7–3, with Roth going the distance. The Gamecocks responded with 3 runs in the second inning in that game against Auburn. They did not even wait that long against the Aggies. A balk, an error and three singles resulted in 4 first-inning runs to quickly pull even with A&M.

As Carolina trotted back out onto the field to begin the second inning, third baseman Adrian Morales scowled as he approached Roth. "I punched Mike in the chest and said, 'Hey, no more runs,'" Morales said. Roth nodded. And he listened. When the left-hander exited the game in the eighth inning, the score was still tied at four. Both Roth and A&M starter Ross Stripling—and the teams' defenses—had calmed significantly after shaky starts.

Roth, in fact, allowed only two hits—a pair of harmless singles—after the first inning. He would have gone longer, but his pitch count had already reached 124 during the eighth inning, and the Gamecocks would obviously need Roth to be fresh later in the tournament. They could not afford to burn him out in the first game. John Taylor and Matt Price picked up where Roth had left off, pitching the final 1⅔ innings perfectly, striking out two.

Fitting the 2011 script, which followed the one from 2010 in Omaha, the team was involved in another tight game. "It did feel a little familiar," Tanner said.

The score was tied 4–4 entering the bottom of the ninth. Scott "Walk-off" Wingo was due up fourth in the inning.

The regional's MVP, Robert Beary, welcomed Aggies reliever Kyle Martin by doubling into the right-field corner. The Gamecocks quickly had the winning run in scoring position with none out.

Bradley had looked rusty in his first three at-bats, but he singled to left field off another new reliever, Nick Fleece. With none out and the top of the order coming up, Holbrook, to be safe, held Beary at third base. Marzilli followed with a walk. The bases were loaded. Wingo was the batter.

Trying to get a ground ball for a double play, the Aggies went to a rather strange alignment. Coach Rob Childress brought in a fifth infielder, leaving only two players in the outfield. If Wingo hit a fly ball, the game would likely be over, anyway. Fleece needed a strikeout or a ground ball.

Wingo played into A&M's hands a bit, falling behind Fleece 1-2. Preparing for a strikeout, ESPN announcers mentioned that Walker, the team's RBI leader, was due up next. Wingo, though, had already been on base four times in four plate appearances. He singled and scored in the first, he singled on a bunt in the second, he doubled to right in the fifth and he was hit by a pitch—extending his school record—in the seventh.

Even behind in the count, he was seeing the ball well. Fleece, a right-hander, wound and fired. He left a fastball up and it tailed back over the plate to the left-handed-hitting Wingo. Wingo squared up the pitch, sending it high and deep toward the right-field corner. It appeared to have the distance for a walk-off grand slam, but it smacked off the wall for a game-winning single.

Beary cruised in with the team's fifth run. Wingo, once again, was a hero. He had gone 4 for 4, been on base five times—and won the game in the bottom of the ninth. "He knew it was his time to go out with a bang," Roth said of Wingo's senior season. "By god if he didn't."

Roth had grown up in the Upstate playing with and against Wingo. "There's certain guys you have a different level of care for," he said. "Scott was one of those guys to me. I hated seeing him hit .200, fight for his job, lose his job. It was so nice to see him get walk-off after walk-off, like I knew he could all along."

Wingo had also ended the Omaha opener drought. The winner's bracket? That was a switch for the Gamecocks. "It's a very unusual feeling for me to be in Omaha and win the first game," Tanner said.

South Carolina had just won its twelfth consecutive NCAA Tournament game and seventh in a row in the College World Series. Roth's NCAA-leading ERA dropped from 1.02 to 0.97.

And Wingo had carved out another chapter in his Carolina legacy. There was still time for more.

Chapter 12
Making Memories

Bayler Teal was every bit the hero of the 2010 College World Series that Whit Merrifield and Michael Roth were. The Gamecocks had fought to stay alive in the tournament, but the idea of survival meant something much different to the Teals. Bayler's eighteen-month war with cancer ended when the seven-year-old died on June 24, 2010, just as South Carolina was in its most trying game on the way to the national championship. As the team grinded to a victory with a twelfth-inning comeback against Oklahoma, Bayler's parents, Risha and Rob, were saying goodbye to their firstborn. Bayler breathed his final breath at 9:32 p.m.

Coach Ray Tanner has repeatedly credited both Bayler and Charlie Peters for providing proper perspective for his team. "We're playing a game," Tanner said. "Are we on the biggest stage in college baseball? Yeah, we all know that. But it's still a game. It's not everything. It's not the end all. Sure, we wanted to get a ring out of it, but is it life and death, that ring? No, not at all. Bayler Teal and Charlie Peters, that's where they've been. That's not where we are."

The Teals were in Omaha for the final two games in 2010. They stood on the field after the team won. They held the NCAA trophy. It was their victory, too.

But soon after, the spotlights dimmed and the attention subsided. Back home in Bishopville, South Carolina, life resumed, and Risha, Rob and five-year-old Bridges had to deal head-on with Bayler's passing. It was difficult, to be sure. The family spent a lot of time at the beach, seeking and praying for clarity and peace. It came in bursts, but then it fizzled. The emptiness of loss can be overwhelming and inescapable.

Bayler left a giant crater in the hearts and minds of the family. He had an oozing personality, even for such a young person. He laughed a bunch and made others do the same. Bridges would sometimes wonder where his best friend was, when he was coming back. His parents got him a tiny little dog named Teddy to help him deal with the loss. Who were they kidding? The pup was just as much for them, something to occupy the idle times when those thoughts of their vibrant son would creep in.

What do you do? How do you move on? Parents are not supposed to outlive their kids. What happens when your oldest doesn't make it to eight years old? The injustice haunts. You feel different, think differently, are treated differently.

The Teals decided later in the year to move to nearby Hartsville, where Risha was from. There were too many memories, too many reminders, of Bayler in the house where he grew up. Some sort of fresh start was needed.

The football season was another pleasant distraction. The Gamecocks had big wins in 2010 against Georgia, Alabama, Florida and Clemson. The morning after the October upset of then number-one Alabama, Risha ran into the bedroom and jumped on the bed.

"Guess what," she said.

"The Gamecocks are on ESPN?" Rob said, energetically.

"No," she said. "Even better."

Risha was pregnant.

The difficulty of the holidays, and Bayler's birthday on Christmas Eve, was smoothed over to some degree by the idea of a little girl growing inside Risha's tummy. Still, the struggle continued. "It's bittersweet," Rob said just before Christmas. "Bayler loved kids so much. You start to get really happy about it, and you stop and think that he would have been happier than anybody."

Rob, once voted the most rabid Gamecocks fan in Lee County, had done the math. Risha would be due in June, near the start of the College World Series. The tournament, even with the championship, had been stained with pain in 2010. What if the new addition came during the 2011 series, providing a new memory to be associated with Omaha?

The 2011 University of South Carolina Baseball Team's Run to Back-to-Back NCAA Championships

Risha was due on June 16, two days before the start of the College World Series and three days before South Carolina's first game in it. June 16 came and went, though, without Risha being in labor. So did the seventeenth and eighteenth. Finally, just before the Gamecocks played Texas A&M, she thought the time had arrived.

The Teals loaded up and drove to Florence, presuming their baby girl would be born overnight. They watched Wingo's walk-off hit against the Aggies on a nine-inch screen. Earlier in the night, they noticed that Roth had Bayler's initials written on his hat, just as he had the year before. Rob had to go up to the television and squint to see the "BT," but the letters were there, black ink on the garnet cap. The tradition had carried on into the next Omaha journey. The gesture made the Teals emotional. "It was so cool to see they were still thinking about him," Rob said.

The baby did not wind up coming that night. A little frustrated and tired, they retreated. The same thing happened the following night. It was another false alarm.

Chad Holbrook's phone buzzed just after 1:00 p.m. on that Tuesday. The team's associate head coach pulled out his smartphone to see a picture of Rob, Risha—and a newborn girl. Piper Teal was born a half hour earlier.

Holbrook smiled and began to tear up. He had always felt especially close to the Teals, considering his own experiences with cancer. Holbrook's oldest son, Reece, was diagnosed with leukemia in 2004. Reece is now in remission, but Holbrook understood the kind of terror the Teals felt in 2010. So that was why he could not contain his emotions when Piper first appeared. "It was so uplifting to see," Holbrook said. "Rob kept telling me to tell people. He was a proud papa."

Piper will always be connected to the brother she will never meet. Her middle name is Joelle. Bayler's middle name was Joel.

"She is beautiful," Rob said hours after she was born, "the most beautiful thing I've ever seen."

Rob is always talkative and energetic, but he was on a whole other level that Tuesday evening. Of course, part of that could have been because the Gamecocks were playing that night in Omaha. Seeing them again in the College World Series stirred emotions in a lot of the team's fans, but nothing like what the Teals were experiencing.

Exactly 363 days removed from losing their son in a hospital room, they were bringing a baby into the world in another one. Both life-changing events coincided with Carolina game days in the College World Series. Or perhaps they weren't mere coincidences.

"It's like a continuation of everything, in a way, but it's different," he said. "It's hard to believe it's been a year. But there are so many good memories, too. And now we're making new good memories."

So were the Gamecocks.

After Wingo's game-winning hit, they were feeling good about themselves—even with number-one seed Virginia on deck. Then again, since when did going against a top-ranked team bother Carolina in any way? Florida and Vanderbilt had already been toppled. The team had eliminated Arizona State, the number-one seed in 2010. What was Virginia to the Gamecocks other than the next victim?

That's the way the game played out, too. A sixty-eight-minute rain delay pushed back the start. When the tarp was pulled, only one team appeared as if it wanted to play. South Carolina scored 6 runs in the first four innings, having no trouble with Virginia in a 7–1 victory that kept the Gamecocks in the winner's bracket. "We played probably one of our better games of the year," Tanner said. "We needed it tonight playing a team the caliber of Virginia. We really probably can't play any better than that."

Christian Walker drove in a pair of runs. Adrian Morales and Brady Thomas, the leaders playing through injuries, had three-hit nights. Cavaliers starter Will Roberts had thrown a perfect game earlier in the season, and he entered the game 11-1 on the year, but he was lifted in the fourth after giving up six runs (three earned) on eight hits.

It was Virginia's second College World Series appearance, with the first coming recently, in 2009, but the Cavs were extremely tight in the early going. They committed three errors despite coming in with a .980 fielding percentage—which was better even than the Gamecocks' defensive rate. Two errors in the first inning, both coming with two outs, were particularly damaging.

Walker reached on a fielding error by third baseman Steven Proscia. Bradley, again in the lineup and batting cleanup against his home state team, doubled to score Walker. Morales then singled, and Bradley scored on a throwing error. Thomas then doubled to plate Morales, and it was 3–0 Gamecocks—mostly because of Virginia generosity. "If I make that play in the first inning, it could have changed the complexion of the game," Proscia said afterward. "It could have been a totally different game."

Then again, perhaps not. Virginia mustered only five hits, scoring on catcher John Hicks's fourth-inning home run off Colby Holmes. Holmes exited two outs shy of earning the victory, turning the game over to sidearm-throwing reliever John Taylor.

The Cavaliers were completely baffled by Taylor's delivery. He went 4⅓ innings, giving up only a hit and a walk. Taylor needed only thirty-four pitches to record thirteen outs, when Holmes had needed ninety-three to go the same distance. In his forty-seventh appearance of the season, Taylor earned his seventh victory. Closer Matt Price came in to retire the final batter, getting Kenny Swab to fly out to Bradley in center field to seal a thorough victory that rivaled that first game at Florida.

The Gamecocks' defense was also excellent in the game. Peter Mooney and Scott Wingo nearly turned a double play for the ages. Wingo stopped a grounder up the middle with his glove and flipped it from behind his back to second base, where Mooney then threw out the runner at first. Only the umpire erroneously called the Cavalier safe at first. It was a close play, but he was out. If there was any doubt, surely Wingo and Mooney's magic deserved the benefit of it.

"The thing about that play is Mooney never saw the bag," Wingo said, still proud months later of its execution. "He just knew where it was, grazed it and got it to Walker. And, let me tell you, that guy was out. He was out. You've got to make that call."

If called correctly, it would have been one of ten double plays for the Gamecocks in the series. Many were completed by that trio of Mooney, Wingo and Walker. "We did it big out there," Wingo said. "We were ready to play. We weren't nervous. We were ready."

South Carolina was 5-2 on the year against number ones, having dropped a game each to Florida and Vanderbilt. "When we were going to play those teams, it didn't matter what they were ranked," Wingo said. "We were the defending champions. So it didn't matter. They had to beat us in Omaha to prove they were better than us. We just had so much confidence."

Virginia eliminated California two days later, setting up a rematch that Friday. The Cavaliers would have to beat the Gamecocks twice to move on to the championships series. It felt far-fetched, but that's precisely what Carolina had done the previous year against rival Clemson. No one was counting out Virginia, especially because the Cavs had held ace Danny Hultzen for their second chance against the Gamecocks.

Chapter 13
Outlasting Virginia

Ray Tanner summed it up sometime after midnight Friday morning in Omaha. "I don't know where to begin," Tanner said, trying and failing to describe the Gamecocks' epic second game against Virginia.

It was difficult to know how to describe it, or where to begin discussing it, because so much happened over the course of four and a half hours. In thirteen innings' worth of baseball, South Carolina should have won and lost several times.

The bottom line is the Gamecocks did eventually win, 3–2, to again advance to the national championship series. But just saying that is selling short what might have been, quite possibly, one of the strangest and best games in the history of the College World Series.

In so many ways, it redefined the sentiments and mantras that had summed up the Gamecocks, really, since the opening month of the season and the March series against Clemson. South Carolina had both jokingly and seriously hung its hat on two phrases—"battle" and "win anyway"—and both were certainly in play in the course of the game that would ultimately eliminate Virginia, the series' top seed.

It wasn't the fact that Carolina won its fifty-third game and got back to the title series as much as it was the how of it all. It was Hollywood stuff. Surely a game like that could not happen in real life. Gamecocks fans had seen varying forms of drama during the 2010 and 2011 seasons but not thirteen innings in the College World Series.

Through three innings, the Gamecocks were figuring out who they were going to throw on Saturday in an elimination game with the

Cavaliers—because ace Danny Hultzen was virtually unhittable. With Hultzen dialed in, there would be no thirteenth inning. This looked as if it would be over quickly, and in nine innings.

The left-hander, the number two overall pick in the draft, was on a different level. Hultzen struck out Evan Marzilli, Scott Wingo and Christian Walker—all swinging—in the first inning. He did the same to Jackie Bradley Jr., Adrian Morales and Brady Thomas in the second. Six up, six down, six strikeouts.

To begin the third, Peter Mooney stroked an 0-2 pitch to center field to break up Hultzen's hypnotism of the Gamecocks. Robert Beary then struck out looking, Jake Williams popped out to short and Marzilli struck out for the second time.

That's when the rumblings began to extend throughout TD Ameritrade Park: something was wrong with Hultzen. Wrong? How? He had been nearly flawless in three innings, if not for a mistake to Mooney that ended in a meaningless single. What could possibly be wrong?

ESPN's crew reported that Hultzen had some strain of the flu. Hultzen sat alone in the Virginia dugout after the third inning, his head buried in a towel he was holding. No one really tended to him, however, and eventually Hultzen walked up the ramp from the dugout.

Kyle Crockett was warming up in the Cavs bullpen. Hultzen, amazingly, was done after those three sterling innings. Down 1–0 at the time, the Gamecocks were both empowered and confused. "I don't know what the guy's deal was," said Michael Roth, Carolina's starter opposite Hultzen. "All I know is Coach Tanner would have to come out there, punch me in the face to knock me out and drag me from the mound to get me off it. It's the College World Series."

For obvious reasons, it was a different game with Hultzen out of it. And Hultzen, despite his illness, did remain in the Virginia dugout. He watched as the Gamecocks scored a pair of runs in the fourth just after his departure. Thomas's one-out double to left scored Walker and Bradley. Even when Hultzen was dealing, Carolina remained upbeat. Connecticut's Matt Barnes as an example, it had hit aces before on the second and third times through the order. "I remember Adrian saying, 'We're fine, we're fine,'" outfielder

Adam Matthews said. "'We'll get some runs on the board.' Everyone was just trying to stay relaxed as possible. I was at the edge of my seat at times." The real drama had not even started yet, either.

The Gamecocks held that 2–1 lead until the eighth inning, the first after Roth walked off having allowed a run on four hits in seven innings. Taylor and Price were being counted on to hold the lead the rest of the way. South Carolina was six outs from making it an all-SEC final. Florida had eliminated Vanderbilt earlier in the day.

For really the only time in the tournament, Carolina's defense hiccupped in that eighth inning. Morales started the frame with a throwing error. A bunt moved leadoff hitter Chris Taylor to second base. Price then entered for John Taylor, immediately getting a much-needed ground ball to Mooney at shortstop.

Mooney, though, had the ball go between his legs and into shallow left-center field. The ghosts of the early SEC season had haunted Mooney at just the wrong time. Chris Taylor scored from second to tie the game at two. So good in 2011 in close and late games, the Gamecocks were having a vulnerable moment. Price responded, getting Steven Proscia to ground into a 4-3 double play, Wingo to Walker at first. South Carolina was out of the inning, but the game was tied. It would stay that way for a while.

After leveling the game, Virginia had the momentum. It continually put runners on against Price, who did not appear to be completely locked in. But the Cavaliers never could manage to score against the All-America closer.

In the ninth: Virginia had the go-ahead run at second base with one out, but Price got a strikeout and a meek foul out.

In the tenth: The Cavaliers had the bases loaded with two out for pinch hitter Reed Gragnani. Price struck him out, swinging, to leave the bases loaded.

In the eleventh: Price pitched around a walk in what was a relatively quiet inning.

In the twelfth: A return to the dramatic tightrope walk for Price. Virginia loaded the bases with one out, but Shane Halley grounded into a double play, Wingo to Walker.

In the thirteenth: The Cavs loaded the bases with none out against Price. Surely this would be the instance in which they would break through for at least a run, if not more. Nope.

Chris Taylor, a tough out, struck out swinging. Then John Barr, who had not hit into a double play all season until the Tuesday game against the Gamecocks, lined a bullet to Wingo. He snared it and flipped to

Mooney, who doubled off Colin Harrington. Price and the Gamecocks had again survived.

Roth and others later teased Price, saying he purposefully got into jams just so he could increase his adrenaline and escape from them. He had made a name for himself in 2010 by getting out of a bases-loaded, zero-out mess during the super regional at Coastal Carolina. Price lived on the edge, no question. But the results were typically solid in the end. The second Clemson game, in which he allowed six runs in less than an inning, was a debacle. He had given up just six runs in his other thirty-two appearances to that point.

Price laughed at the halfhearted accusation that he intentionally allowed base runners only to heroically mow down subsequent batters. He could have fooled anyone in his 5⅔ innings, in which he pitched around twelve base runners (seven hits, five walks). "Looking back," he said, "how in the world did I get through that?"

Through the top of the thirteenth, Price had thrown ninety-five pitches—four more than Roth had. He was hopeful of a conclusion but physically felt as if he could go all night. "I didn't feel my arm at all," he said months later. "My arm felt great. Once the adrenaline starts going, you don't feel anything at all. You just want to go out there, throw as hard as you can and get everybody out. That adrenaline takes over your game."

And to think, Tanner and pitching coach Jerry Meyers wondered before and during the season whether Price would have enough value as the team's closer. They considered moving him to the starting rotation as late as March, ultimately leaving him on the back end.

Price had seven victories and eighteen saves. Plenty of value in those numbers.

"It didn't surprise me because of what he did throughout the year," Meyers said of the performance. "It's one of those deals where you prepare all year for the unexpected and handling whatever's going to be thrown at you and giving your best effort. He was ready for that. I think that gave us an edge as a team, even though the game was in the balance."

Price had battled, plainly put. He said he was tired afterward. That's fair, right? And the extra innings were as emotionally draining as they were physically.

"There is a lot of pressure," he said. "I really block it all out. I think, 'I've been doing this, pitching, for a long time. I've done all the work to get into this situation, my whole career.' Then you just have to find a way, get outs."

Price and South Carolina had repeatedly prevented Virginia from winning the game, but the Gamecocks still had to win it themselves. They'd had five base runners in extra innings, but like Virginia, they had failed to come through with the big hit at the opportune time.

At least Carolina had outlasted Virginia closer Branden Kline, who ran out of fuel after five innings. The Cavaliers called on right-hander Cody Winiarski to pitch the bottom of the thirteenth. Winiarski, a senior pitching his last game, never recorded an out.

Thomas led off the inning with a single to center field. Tanner turned to Matthews and asked if he could pinch run. Matthews's mind said no—his hamstring was still bothering him—but his heart and mouth said yes. Mooney got down a bunt, trying to advance Matthews to second base. Matthews was not full speed as he proceeded, and Winiarski felt as if he had a chance to throw out the lead runner. The throw, though, sailed wide and into center field. Matthews was easily safe at second. He said he initially wanted to run to third, but he held, recognizing how detrimental it would be if he were thrown out.

Beary was far from Carolina's best bunter, but it made sense for him to attempt to move Matthews to third. With the way things were playing out, the bunt might also put more pressure on Virginia's defense. Beary made awkward contact, nudging the ball back out toward Winiarski. The pitcher again tried to make the hero play instead of the sure one, spinning and firing wildly toward third base. The ball glanced off Proscia's foot and into the field's expansive foul territory.

Matthews, sliding into the base, had no idea where the ball was. He froze. Then, all he heard was third base coach Chad Holbrook hollering for him to run home. "Coach Holbrook was going, 'go, go, go,'" Matthews said. "I just had to listen to him and trust him. I didn't even look back to see the ball."

Matthews sprinted toward the plate. He made it without a throw. The Gamecocks had a weird walk-off win.

It had been a rough, fruitless season for Matthews in a lot of ways, but he touched the plate to end a very trying game. "It's one of the highlights of my career, personally," Matthews said. "It was a lot of fun and kind of crazy how it worked out."

Matthews had played in thirty-four games his junior season, but he scored the game-winning run in two significant instances: the Virginia game in Omaha and the series-clinching victory at Florida. Matthews and the Gamecocks were about to get the Gators again in another best-of-three. The winner this time, though, would lay claim to the national championship.

Virginia coach Brian O'Connor was biased because Carolina had eliminated his talented team. But he essentially said he would not bet against the Gamecocks. He had seen this story play out before. Oregon State was the last team to win consecutive NCAA titles, in 2006 and 2007. That's what Carolina looked like, to O'Connor.

"Obviously, South Carolina has got something very, very special going on right now," said O'Connor, whose team lost twelve times all year but twice in four days to the Gamecocks. "It just seems like they just find a way."

A way to…win anyway?

Several times during the game, and especially during the extra innings, Charlie Peters's vision shot toward the sky. His parents had taught him to pray, and these jams seemed like good times for some help from above. At one point, Tanner asked him what he was praying for.

"A double play," Peters told the coach.

Peters was 8-0 since kindling his relationship with the team in 2010. The Gamecocks saw him as a magical sort of kid. He took the role seriously. "There's a lot of pressure on you," he earnestly said. "You don't want to let them down."

His prayers for double plays were answered, but the players were curious if Charlie would implore the heavens for a run so everyone could go home. "Once we'd get out of a jam," he said, "everyone would say, 'Charlie, you've got to get us some runs.'" Charlie would nod.

After the top of the thirteenth and Price's ultimate Houdini act—with the help of his middle infield—Charlie could not hold it anymore. He simply had to go to the bathroom.

As he walked back down the ramp to the dugout, he saw Matthews go streaking across his line of sight to score the winning run. Charlie was 9-0. The Gamecocks had won their fourteenth consecutive NCAA Tournament game, a new record.

Two more victories in Omaha and they would join an elite club of back-to-back champions. Only four schools had done it previously.

Chapter 14
Breaking News

South Carolina had earned some rest before the championship series against Florida. Sure, the Gamecocks had played just three games in six days, but how exhausting were the walk-off wins against Texas A&M and Virginia? It felt as if they had played two games against the Cavaliers on that Friday night—and really, they had played one and a half games.

It could have been worse, though. If Virginia had broken through in any of those bases-loaded situations in the extra innings, there would have been an elimination game on Saturday night. "We definitely didn't want to play Saturday," said starter Michael Roth, who pitched seven innings against Virginia before the game was finally decided in the thirteenth. The Gamecocks could rest and reset their pitching to face Florida, which was probably the deepest staff in the College World Series. Price, who had thrown ninety-five pitches in $5\frac{2}{3}$ innings on Friday, was unlikely to be ready by Monday. For Roth to appear in the series, it would either have to go three games or he would pitch in game two on three days' rest.

In addition to pitching $14\frac{1}{3}$ innings in his two College World Series starts, Roth had been dealing with something of an off-field firestorm—of his own creation. The night before the team's first game in Omaha, which was also Father's Day eve, Roth wanted to give a shoutout to his dad, David. "How's this for dedication?" Roth said on Twitter. "My dad had to quit his job to make it out to Omaha."

To Roth, it was a thoughtful gesture that he wanted to acknowledge. David Roth had missed his son's starts against Clemson and UCLA in the

2010 series, mostly because they were not anticipated—but also because he could not spontaneously take vacation days. "My wife told me that being in the stands for the championship games was unlike anything she'd ever experienced," David said, referring to Michael's mother, Deborah.

In 2011, Michael had turned into one of the best pitchers in college baseball. There would be no surprise starts for him; he was the team's frontline guy. "There was no way I was going to be home watching the games," his dad said. "I had to be in Omaha to support Michael this time. Getting to Omaha once was amazing. I never dreamed they would be there two years in a row."

Michael said his dad is the one often hounding him about homework, so it was an added bonus for him to see Michael claim the Elite 88 award as the top scholar in college baseball.

To be there, though, David did have to walk away from his job as a salesman at Steve White Volkswagen in Greenville. Michael said his dad left the company on good terms. Passionate South Carolina fans, however, were outraged when they learned he was not allowed to go see his son pitch in Omaha. That fervor spiked when national publications and websites, including Yahoo! and Huffington Post, picked up the story. Over the course of the week, the car dealership received dozens of phone calls, hate mail and Michael thought maybe even a bomb threat.

"I don't necessarily regret it, because it's something that happened," Michael said. "I am sorry the car dealership caught as much as it did. I know I just thought it was awesome my dad was able to go and make such a commitment and my mom blessed it."

The rest of the family could laugh about it later, but it still bothered David, whom Michael has always said is a rather shy person—the antithesis of Michael, in other words. David wanted the series to be about his son and the Gamecocks, not him and his job situation. "I didn't like it," he said. "To me, it was a private matter. Neither of us was prepared for what happened."

He said he was embarrassed by the attention. Some reporters essentially stalked him at games, asking for interviews. David said he was regrettably short with some of them after a while. "I hated having Michael, his teammates and coaches bothered by the attention of it all," he said. "As I look back, I only find it was a lousy experience."

Eventually, the paparazzi subsided, and the focus went back toward Roth on the mound. If he did not know it already, Michael learned the power of social media. "It's a powerful tool," he said. "It's something I've kind of embraced."

Assistant Chad Holbrook (@cholbrook2) was really the first of the Gamecocks to regularly use Twitter. After the 2010 season, more and more players took to it. Jackie Bradley Jr. (@JackieBradleyJr) was the early leader among the players. Soon, Roth (@mtroth29) appeared. Suddenly, there were dozens. Roth is so invested that he even put his Twitter handle on his glove after the 2011 season, but Ray Tanner put the kibosh on that.

"The players, we were already close, but it kept us talking to each other even when we weren't around one another," Roth said. "It allowed us to interact with each other and the fans. Then fans felt closer to us, on a personal level. They felt like they were part of the team."

David Roth eventually landed a job at another car dealership, though he had to be discerning in making sure he did not receive the job because of the story and his connection to Gamecocks baseball. Everything was on the up and up. Michael suspected that his dad's new bosses will be more lenient should Carolina return to Omaha in 2012. "I'm sure it won't be a problem after last year," he said.

One thing was guaranteed by the day before the championship series began: a Southeastern Conference team was again going to win.

Louisiana State was the 2009 champion, followed by Carolina in 2010. It would be an SEC East team in 2011, either the Gamecocks or the Gators. "We feel like the SEC is certainly the best conference in the country," Florida coach Kevin O'Sullivan said during the championship series news conference.

The Gators were probably the most talented in the country, but the Gamecocks were far from the underdogs they continued to advertise themselves as being. After all, they had already defeated Florida in a road series in 2011. The series really was a tossup. "If you want to look on paper, they might beat us position for position every time," Roth said, "but when you look at the mental aspect, we really had the edge."

But then bits and pieces of damaging information started to trickle from Carolina's camp. First baseman Christian Walker, the team's top hitter and run-producer, was dealing with some sort of injury. What? How serious? Could he play against the Gators? Those were the questions that hung in the air through the weekend and even into Monday.

Two weeks before the 2011 season, catcher Brady Thomas was granted a sixth year by the NCAA. The captain was third on the team with a .316 batting average. *Courtesy of Paul Collins.*

Junior center fielder Jackie Bradley Jr. was a preseason All-America selection after a 2010 season in which he was the Most Outstanding Player of the College World Series. *Courtesy of Paul Collins.*

Christian Walker started the 2011 season on a rampage. The sophomore first baseman hit four home runs and drove in fifteen runs in the first nine games of the season. *Courtesy of Paul Collins.*

Scott Wingo and Jake Williams teamed up to help the Gamecocks win early season games against Georgia and Clemson. Williams, a Wofford transfer, hit a key three-run home run to defeat Clemson. *Courtesy of Paul Collins.*

Junior college transfer Peter Mooney committed seven errors in his first sixteen games as a Gamecock, but the shortstop settled down to become a defensive star in the second half of the season. *Courtesy of Paul Collins.*

Senior captain Scott Wingo evolved in his final year at the plate. Beginning with the March 19 game against Georgia, Wingo supplied his team with four game-winning hits in 2011. *Courtesy of Paul Collins.*

A junior college coach suggested Florence native John Taylor begin pitching with a sidearm delivery. It eventually paid off with a fifty-appearance senior season at Carolina. *Courtesy of Paul Collins*.

Sometimes pitchers bat in the Major Leagues, but it rarely happens in the college game. All-America closer Matt Price had to hack, though, against Vanderbilt. He struck out, but Carolina won the game. *Courtesy of Paul Collins*.

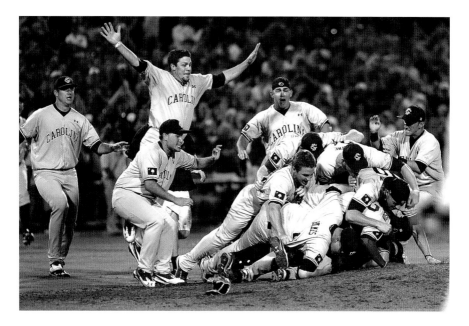

For the first time since 2004, South Carolina hosted—and won—a home super regional. After defeating Connecticut in two close games, the Gamecocks advanced to the tenth College World Series in the program's history. *Courtesy of Paul Collins.*

The 2011 season marked the fifth time Ray Tanner had taken South Carolina to the College World Series. The veteran coach had a full speaking circuit following his first title. *Courtesy of Paul Collins.*

Omaha shifted from Rosenblatt Stadium to the new TD Ameritrade Park for the 2011 College World Series. The event moved to the $131 million downtown ballpark after sixty years in the south Omaha neighborhood. *Courtesy of Paul Collins.*

Omaha native Charlie Peters (left) first met the Gamecocks in 2003, when he was battling cancer. By the 2011 College World Series, a healthy Peters was asked to be the team's batboy. *Courtesy of Paul Collins.*

Junior Michael Roth was a left-handed specialist in 2010, but he emerged to become one of the top starting pitchers in college baseball in 2011. Roth won fourteen games and had a 1.06 ERA. *Courtesy of Paul Collins.*

Against long odds, junior center fielder Jackie Bradley Jr. returned from a wrist injury in time for the College World Series. Injured April 23, Bradley recovered weeks ahead of schedule. *Courtesy of Paul Collins.*

South Carolina was the last champion at Rosenblatt Stadium. It vowed to return for the opening of the new stadium, TD Ameritrade Park, and the Gamecocks achieved that goal. *Courtesy of Paul Collins.*

Junior ace pitcher Michael Roth was surprised to learn upon arrival that his picture adorned billboards all over the Omaha area, including the side of TD Ameritrade Park. *Courtesy of Paul Collins.*

South Carolina had lost seven consecutive College World Series openers until it defeated Texas A&M to begin the 2011 tournament. *Courtesy of Paul Collins.*

Carolina closer Matt Price battled again and again through difficult positions, some of which were his own doing. Price led the nation with twenty saves. *Courtesy of Paul Collins.*

The Gamecocks again succeeded because of strong defense in the field. Second baseman Scott Wingo was an important part of the team's nine double plays in the College World Series. *Courtesy of Paul Collins.*

Pitching coach Jerry Meyers rejoined the Carolina staff after six years away as Old Dominion's head coach. Meyers's staff had a 2.45 ERA, allowing for a seamless transition from Mark Calvi. *Courtesy of Paul Collins.*

Head coach Ray Tanner had been to Omaha three times with the Gamecocks before they broke through in 2010 to win the national title. Tanner did not have to wait nearly as long to claim his second. *Courtesy of Paul Collins.*

Of South Carolina's five victories in the 2011 College World Series, closer Matt Price won two games and saved two more. He was on the mound for 5 $^2/_3$ innings in the 13-inning victory against Virginia. *Courtesy of Paul Collins.*

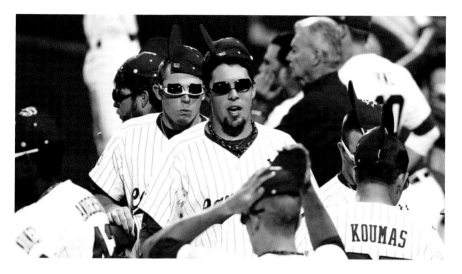

South Carolina sometimes needed some help from the baseball gods to get victories. Outfielder Adam Matthews and pitcher Michael Roth demonstrate proper fashion sacrifices. *Courtesy of Paul Collins.*

Second baseman Scott Wingo was a career .226 hitter in his first three seasons, but he turned himself into the College World Series' Most Outstanding Player as a senior. *Courtesy of Paul Collins.*

If Florida's Cody Dent crossed the plate against the Gamecocks, the Gators would have won the first of the best-of-three championship series. Jake Williams fired home to catcher Robert Beary… *Courtesy of Paul Collins.*

…and Beary just did get Dent at the plate. The game continued, and Carolina won in the eleventh inning in what was its thirteenth one-run victory of the year. *Courtesy of Paul Collins.*

For the second consecutive season, South Carolina's season ended with a championship—and a traditional dog pile on the Omaha soil. Batboy Charlie Peters is reluctant to join initially. *Courtesy of Paul Collins*.

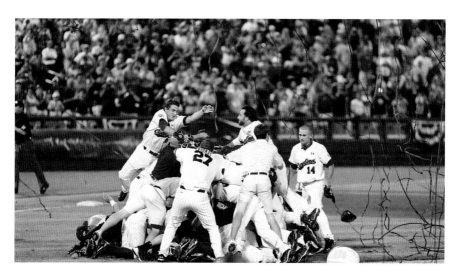

The Gamecocks finished the year 55-14, setting NCAA records for consecutive games won in the NCAA Tournament (16) and the College World Series (11), going back to the 2010 season. *Courtesy of Paul Collins*.

The city of Columbia again welcomed home the NCAA champions like kings. The university flag flew atop the State House as thousands gathered for a parade down Main Street. *Courtesy of Paul Collins.*

McBee's McLeod Farms honored the Gamecocks a few months after the second national championship by cutting a team-themed corn maze into the land. *Courtesy of Paul Collins.*

The 2011 University of South Carolina Baseball Team's Run to Back-to-Back NCAA Championships

Walker had sixty-two runs batted in, nineteen more than anyone on the team. He was batting about twenty points higher than anyone, just shy of .350. With Bradley working his way back following a two-month layoff, there was no question who had carried the Carolina offense in 2011.

And the sophomore was hurt. Going thirteen innings to defeat Virginia had taxed the Gamecocks' pitching staff to some extent, but there was another cost. Carolina fans were probably unhappy with Walker after his innocuous at-bat in the bottom of the twelfth inning. With none out and Evan Marzilli on second and Scott Wingo on first, Walker flied out to right field. It was a scoreless inning and a missed chance for the Gamecocks, who won in the next inning.

Walker remembered swinging through a curveball for a strike. It was an awkward swing. He stepped out of the batter's box, collected himself and hit the next pitch to the right fielder. Walker ran out the fly ball, and he recalled feeling something strange as he turned to head back toward the dugout. It felt worse and worse with each step. His left hand was starting to throb.

"As soon as I stepped back in the dugout, the pain was crazy," said Walker, who immediately sought out trainer Brainard Cooper. Cooper pushed and prodded at Walker's hand, trying to determine the nature and severity of the injury. He would move it in certain ways that made Walker wince. Once, he audibly indicated his level of pain.

Cooper looked up at Walker. "I'm pretty sure it's your hamate," he said.

That was a dreaded word in the vernacular of South Carolina baseball. Bradley had lost about the first month of the 2010 season after fracturing the bone, which is located in the palm. Bradley returned quickly but still required surgery. The Gamecocks had two or three games left—the most important games of the season.

Cooper asked Walker if he could finish the game against Virginia. He said he could and did, though he did not have to make a defensive play or bat in the thirteenth inning.

The following day, Saturday, the Gamecocks had an indoor workout. Walker watched. Cooper had told him not to do a thing. Roth walked up to him during the practice. "You going to play?" he asked Walker. Walker nodded. "Yeah," Roth said, "you better."

"They expected me to play," Walker said. But there was a lot of doubt as to whether he would. A lot would be determined during a Sunday afternoon batting practice at TD Ameritrade Park. Walker wore a "little" wrist brace similar to one that Bradley had after his return in 2010. He was standing around the cage when Cooper and Tanner asked Walker to take a swing.

"The bat almost flew out of my hand," Walker said. "It was the worst pain I've ever felt."

At that point, Tanner accepted that he would not have his best offensive player for the championship series. "No question," he said. "I understand hamates. I've seen enough of them, had a few of them on my teams. You can't play through it. Once the fracture is confirmed, it's going to be four to six weeks, best-case scenario."

Tanner had mentally moved on. "I watched him go to his knees. I said, 'Okay, I guess we'll adjust, try to figure out a lineup.'"

Unable to swing, Walker made his way to the dugout. He plopped down, looking at his left hand. "I was pretty much 100 percent that I wasn't going to play," Walker said. "Mentally and emotionally, not even dealing with the pain, I couldn't help but wonder, 'Why now?' I had played all year and helped my team get to that point. The day before the championship series, and then that happens? It was tough to deal with, but at the same time I didn't want to tell myself I wasn't playing. I wanted to keep some kind of hope. I didn't want to count myself out completely."

His teammates' hearts ached for him. They tried not to be fearful about their chances against Florida without him, laboring to show that same resiliency, but this was by far the team's best hitter. "You could almost see some tears come to his eyes," Bradley said. "It was the middle of the College World Series. We were right where we wanted to be. It kind of took the air out of us. It definitely took it out of him."

Walker would need surgery. There was no way around that. But could it wait? Was there anything that could be medically done to mask and alleviate the crippling pain? Walker went to dinner that night with his parents, discussing those topics and whether there were any answers. He said he was "pretty devastated" by the predicament.

As he rode back to the team's hotel, the Marriott in west Omaha, he received a call from Tanner. He wanted to meet with him upon arrival. So Walker and his mother sat with Tanner and Cooper in the hotel lobby, hashing out what Monday's plan would be. He would get an X-ray exam in the morning and the team would fly its physicians, Chris Mazoue and John

Walsh, to see him. They were going to pull out all the stops, at least giving Walker every opportunity to play.

Walker and Cooper went very early that Monday morning—hours before the first championship game—to an Omaha hospital, where they learned it was a fracture of his left hamate bone. While Mazoue and Walsh traveled, Cooper administered a variety of treatments. "Anything Brainard could think of," Walker said, "we tried it." When the doctors did arrive, they tried some theories of their own. They believed Walker was not risking further injury, but they did not really know how to quell the pain.

The doctors continued to work with Walker during the team's batting practice. During it, Steven Neff and Roth took grounders at first base. Neff had never played first base in college, to anyone's knowledge; he was just athletic. Roth, the ace with thirteen victories, was starting and batting ninth in the original, Walker-less lineup. The alternatives were far from ideal.

Adrian Morales at one point saw Walker, looked sternly at him and said, "You know you're playing. There's no way you're sitting out of this game." But Walker didn't know. It had been a long forty-eight hours. "It was pretty suspenseful, not knowing."

Finally, the doctors looked at Walker and said they had done all they could. The only way to know if the hand would hold up was for him to take some swings in the cage. He would have his own batting practice session, with thousands filing into the stadium to watch. There was hope, but not a lot, as Walker stepped into the batter's box. At least he had progressed enough to make it that far. If it did not work out, Walker and the medical staff had given it their best shot. Maybe they could try again the next day or the following day, if there was a third game.

Tanner's expectations were incredibly low as the first pitch was delivered. Walker seemed to swing all right. He certainly did not go down to his knees, as he had the previous days. He was not in too much pain from what he saw.

Walker said he did not know where the ball went. It just got over the wall in left field. Without realizing it, he had homered in his first swing. Walker seemed to be feeling fine. He hit four more home runs during the batting practice, the last sailing over the 375-foot mark in left-center field. Tanner had to pick up his jaw from the dirt beneath him.

"I could not believe that. I was baffled," Tanner said. "I was standing right next to that cage, going, 'Are you serious?' I didn't understand how it was happening. After he hit the first one, after one swing, I asked if he just wanted to shut it down and go with that. I was sold with that."

Impressive as Bradley's comeback was, this was on a different plane. Bradley knew, especially, since he had felt that same pain the previous year. "I could barely even hold a pencil," Bradley said. "For him to tough it out, that's still really amazing to me. For him to go through that, I honestly don't know how he did that. I told him, 'I promise you that you will not be able to swing a bat.' I was wrong, and I'm glad I was wrong."

Two of Tanner's top stars, Bradley and Walker, had demonstrated something bordering on miraculous in Omaha. After Walker hit, Tanner went to the dugout and made a new lineup. Bradley and Walker were respectively hitting second and third, playing center field and first base. It was business as usual, despite all odds.

"You go through the whole Walker thing and you think, 'My goodness,'" Tanner said. "Their toughness exceeds what you can imagine, for me. I've been doing this a long time. It was amazing, for me. No matter what all has happened, in my entire athletic life—playing or coaching—the fact Walker got back involved in the College World Series is incredible to me."

Walker's plan: gut through two games, get home with another trophy and have surgery.

Chapter 15

Celebrating Again

As experienced of a coach as Ray Tanner was, he was still fighting anxious energy when he arrived that Monday afternoon at TD Ameritrade Park. It was the third time his South Carolina teams had played for a national championship, and the second in as many years, but nerves would have invaded even if he had been part of three hundred national title games.

Wrestling with the anxiety, he decided to go out to the dugout, get some air and clear his head. Tanner walked down the ramp, turned the corner—and saw Charlie Peters sitting there on the bench with a glove. Peters looked up and smiled at Tanner.

Everything else disappeared. "It was like a sigh of relief," Tanner said. "We chatted, just me and Charlie. It's been wonderful to have that kind of experience with young people like that. It does put it in perspective; we're playing a game."

Good thing Charlie was there to calm Tanner, because the game that evening against Florida would have sent him into fits of stress. The fact that it was anywhere near the level of the second Virginia game demonstrated that it was another classic.

The Gamecocks would again have to deal with Florida ace Hudson Randall, who had shut them down in a March 26 complete game—their only loss in the series to the Gators. Randall was demonstrating similar mastery on the big stage in Omaha. He had allowed only two hits entering the eighth inning. "I see him in my sleep," Tanner said.

One, though, was a double in the first inning by Christian Walker—the same Walker who did not know until minutes before the game whether he would play due to the broken bone in his left hand. Walker sent the first pitch he saw from Randall down the right field line, cruising into second base with his twenty-first double of the season as if nothing were wrong. "That was awesome," Carolina second baseman Scott Wingo said of Walker's hit. "I'll never forget it. It didn't matter, hurt or whatever, we were going to give it all we had."

The two-out double did no harm after Brady Thomas grounded out, and Randall settled into a seemingly unshakable rhythm. Following a two-out single in the fourth inning, the six-foot, three-inch right-hander retired ten consecutive hitters, striking out three of them. No one was seeing Randall well, and the team was running out of at-bats.

Carolina's pitching was doing its best to keep the Gamecocks in the game. Freshman Forrest Koumas did not appear rattled by his first College World Series start. Koumas had not pitched since the June 5 regional-sealing victory against Stetson. Just like he had in Gainesville, though, he did his best to match Randall.

The Gators scratched across a run in the third on a walk, a ground ball, a wild pitch and a sacrifice fly. That is all Koumas allowed, though, in 5⅔ innings. Tyler Webb, who began the season in the starting rotation, then came on for 2⅓ important scoreless innings in relief.

Down 1–0, the Gamecocks had not given up, but how would they hit Randall? The sophomore just cracked the door open to begin the eighth, walking Peter Mooney to begin the inning. Robert Beary was then able to get down a bunt to push Mooney into scoring position with one out. With only five outs to play with, it represented Carolina's best—and probably last—chance that night against the Gators. Leadoff man Evan Marzilli got into a hitter's count, ahead 2-0, but then he flied out to center field. The ball was hit deep enough, though, to get Mooney to third base. He stood ninety feet from tying the game at 1.

That brought up Wingo. Randall left a 2-2 curveball up in the strike zone, and Wingo did what he had all season, coming through with a single to center field. The ball caromed off the mound, under Randall's glove and then just got past second baseman Josh Adams's diving attempt at it. Mooney trotted in with the tying run. Wingo's hit was just as important, in some senses, as any of his walk-offs from the year.

Wingo had batted near the bottom of the order virtually his entire Carolina career until April. Tanner moved him up to second, and he never let go of it.

The 2011 University of South Carolina Baseball Team's Run to Back-to-Back NCAA Championships

Back in the fall, Tanner let Wingo "coach" one of the teams in the Garnet and Black World Series intrasquad scrimmages, which meant he could make his own lineup. Wingo batted himself fourth. Tanner laughed and rolled his eyes. But then Wingo went something like nine for ten and drove in half his team's runs in the three scrimmages.

Turned out, he really did belong in the top third of the lineup. "He'll walk. He'll get hit by a pitch. He'll move a runner. He'll bunt for a base hit," Tanner said. "He's a consummate team guy. That's the kind of guy you've got to have in the 2 hole, a very unselfish player that's team-oriented."

That was Wingo. Without that hit, it's likely the Gamecocks would have lost 1–0 and been behind 1-0 in the series. Instead, they had new life, playing in another tie game in the late innings.

After thirteen innings the previous Friday, what were the Gamecocks in store for against the Gators?

Closer Matt Price was not expected to be available, since he had thrown ninety-five pitches. Price had done everything he could all weekend to rest and recover, just in case, but it would be a lot to ask of a reliever to essentially come back on two days' rest after throwing more pitches than the starter did in the game.

Without him, the late-inning lights would shine on John Taylor. The senior from Florence was making his forty-ninth appearance of the year, two shy of the NCAA single-season record. Throwing sidearm, he said, kept his right arm a bit fresher than if he were an overhand pitcher. So the amount of work had not fatigued him by late June.

Taylor failed in an early bid to be the team's closer in 2010, eventually ceding that gig to Price. In 2011, though, he proved his worth as a setup man. Pitching coach Jerry Meyers gushed about Taylor's importance to the 2011 team's success, as evidenced by the number of games in which he pitched. "He felt like he was better than he was the year before," Meyers said. "He was going to leave nothing to chance going into his senior season and his last opportunity."

Taylor finished the season with a 1.14 earned-run average, even with all those appearances. He was 8-1. He allowed nine earned runs in $71\frac{1}{3}$ innings.

He had apparently been taking cues from Price, however, in terms of getting himself in trouble. Taylor started the ninth inning by walking SEC Offensive Player of the Year Mike Zunino. Brian Johnson then singled to right field, moving Zunino to third base. Taylor then intentionally walked Adams, loading the bases with none out.

If Zunino crossed the plate, the game would be over. The percentages of Taylor preventing that were incredibly low. Then again, he had seen Price do it repeatedly, as if it were not all that difficult.

Left fielder Tyler Thompson got the end of the bat on an 0-2 pitch from Taylor, grounding it toward the right side of the infield. Wingo was drawn in so he could make a throw to the plate and prevent Zunino from scoring to win the game. He had to dive to his right, toward second base. Wingo snared the ball. He quickly got to his feet and fired toward the plate. But he rushed the throw. It was off line, heading toward the dirt just in front of the left-hander's batter's box.

Catcher Robert Beary, who had taken over for Thomas late in the season, kept his right foot on home plate as he leaned as far as he could up the first-base line. Wingo's throw took an awkward short hop just in front of his outstretched mitt.

This was a play Walker made at first base all the time, on poor throws from the other infielders. But with a catcher's mitt? The dynamics of the glove are so significantly different.

But Beary made the play. The ball jumped up into the mitt and stuck. Zunino was sliding in behind him as he squeezed the ball into the glove. If Beary had dropped it, the game would have been over. He held on.

"I've never practiced it. I'd never tried it," Beary said. "You just do it. You might have a better chance with a first baseman's glove or outfield glove. It was just a natural reaction. The Lord wanted it to go that way." Beary said he might make the play eight out of ten times with a different glove. "With a catcher's mitt," he said, "it might be half that—if that."

So many things about the play were abnormal. Well, they would have been for most teams, anyway. "Really, I think God was looking down on us, smiling or something—or playing a joke on Florida," Michael Roth said.

There was still only one out, and the bases were still loaded. The Gamecocks were far from out of danger.

Bill Wingo was nervously pacing around the concourse. He said the situation reminded him of all the practices with Scott when he was a Little Leaguer. They would dream up scenarios like this on the neighborhood field: Bottom of the ninth. Bases loaded. Have to throw out the runner at home.

Now it was all happening in real life. "This is when you've got to want the ball coming to you," said Bill Wingo, the former Clemson infielder. "I said, 'Hit him another one.'"

Sure enough, Daniel Pigott did just that. He meekly grounded the 0-1 pitch from Taylor directly to Wingo—no diving necessary this time—and Wingo threw cleanly to Beary, setting up Beary's throw to get Pigott at first.

It was a 4-2-3 double play for the second and third outs of the ninth inning, and Carolina had somehow escaped. How many lives did these Gamecocks have? Pigott stood just past first base with his hands on his hips. He could not believe what had just happened. Not many people could.

"To see him make those two plays, I said, 'My gosh,'" Bill Wingo said of his son, who was saving the Gamecocks at every turn. "It was unbelievable. I said, 'We're going to win this game.'"

Maybe. But not before some additional drama.

Carolina put two on with one out in the tenth inning, after Jake Williams and Beary both singled. But Marzilli struck out looking, and Wingo proved he was actually human with a groundout to strand two runners.

Taylor again struggled in the bottom of the tenth, allowing a leadoff single by Cody Dent. Nolan Fontana moved Dent to second with a bunt. Bryson Smith flied to left for the second out of the inning. The Carolina coaches then opted to walk the left-handed-hitting Preston Tucker to get to Zunino. The Gamecocks would have the righty-on-righty matchup but, then again, they would not have the advantage—because Zunino hit .371 with nineteen home runs in 2011. Forget a home run; a single would have more than likely scored Dent from second. It was not as if South Carolina had Major League arms in the outfield.

Zunino roped the first pitch from Taylor into left field, where Williams knew he would have to collect the ball quickly and make the throw of his life to Beary. Dent had decent speed and was moving on contact, since there were two outs.

Williams scooped the ball perfectly, set his feet and launched his whole body into the heave toward the plate. It did not quite make it there. Beary had to scurry up the third-base line to cut off the throw, but he was only about a foot or two from the base line when the ball arrived—and Dent was not yet by Beary.

Beary received Williams's throw to the left side of his body. He instantly twisted and reached the mitt toward Dent, who was trying to skirt Beary's advance. Beary just got the mitt on Dent's right side. Beary leapt to his feet and held the baseball high in the air.

Dent was out. The inning was over.

Williams and Beary, bench players for the bulk of the season, had prevented the Gamecocks from losing the series' pivotal first game. "Jake couldn't throw the ball twenty yards," center fielder Jackie Bradley Jr. said, "and he makes the throw of his life against Florida. It's crazy how everything laid into place."

Looking for more comfort in tense times, Tanner said he would talk with Charlie like he had before the game. "That was my escape," Tanner said. "I'd say, 'What are you thinking here, big guy?'" They'd start laughing as Charlie tentatively offered his solution to the situation. "It was fun having him there."

The players continued to tease Charlie, as they had against Virginia, to get them some runs. Finally, in the top of the eleventh inning, the Gamecocks broke through with one.

Walker, playing with that broken hand, scored it. He stuck a one-out single into center field for his second hit of the night. During Adam Matthews's pinch-hit at-bat, Tanner signaled for Walker—despite the injury—to steal second base. It was the art of deception at its finest. Florida knew Walker was limited; it would never expect him to steal second.

He got a big jump on reliever Greg Larson and Zunino. Zunino, caught off guard and perhaps affected by a late swing from Matthews, made a terrible throw that sailed wide and well over Adams's glove and into center field. It was just his third error of the season.

Walker, who has at best average speed, got up and headed for third base. Florida's Smith thought he had a chance to get Walker at third. Smith's throw sank right at the base, and it ricocheted into the Gators' dugout. Walker jogged in with the go-ahead run to make it 2–1 in a play that was somewhat similar to how the Virginia game had ended, when Matthews scored as a result of a pair of errors.

As the half-inning continued, Tanner and Meyers called to the bullpen to see if they could somehow get an inning out of Price. By the time they got on the phone, Price was already warming up.

Price gave up a leadoff hit to Johnson, and a pinch runner got into scoring position with a bunt. But Price rallied to strike out Thompson and induce a Pigott groundout to Mooney at short. Price had save number nineteen and South Carolina had a 2–1 victory, its thirteenth and final one-run win in 2011.

The Gamecocks had played two of the more memorable games in the history of the College World Series in consecutive outings. They had won both. And they were one victory away from their second national title in a row.

Carolina would have Roth on the mound on three days' rest. Some suggested saving the team's ace another day for the potential deciding game, but Roth would not stand for it. This was the same player who had demanded the ball to begin the SEC Tournament. Roth had started on three days' rest against UCLA in the game that determined the championship. He was hopeful of similar results.

Roth aside, how would Florida respond in the second game? The Gators had game one in hand several times, only to see the Gamecocks dramatically hold on to win in eleven innings. If they got behind early, would they fold to those wearing garnet pinstripes?

Wingo drove in the game's first run with a sacrifice fly to right field. Then the Gators' defense let the team down. Florida shortstop Nolan Fontana successfully made 289 defensive plays in 2011, but two of his twelve miscues came against the Gamecocks. A Fontana fielding error allowed them to tie the rubber game in Gainesville. In Omaha, Walker hit a two-out chopper that kicked high in the air off Fontana's glove and landed in shallow center field. Marzilli scored, and Thomas then singled in Bradley. Carolina had staked Roth to an early 3–0 lead.

The team's coaches and trainers were not sure if Walker would be able to play that Tuesday because his hand had swollen significantly overnight. After another long day of treatment, he was again in the lineup—and again contributing. Walker was on base four times in the series' second game, including two more hits. Roth said the team felt "invincible" having Walker on the field, despite his broken hamate bone. "Nothing was stopping us," Roth said.

Zunino hit a leadoff homer off him in the fourth inning, but Roth was still standing on the mound with a 4–1 lead in the eighth inning. A Mooney home run—the only one for the Gamecocks in the College World Series and their forty-sixth and final one of the season—to start the sixth inning pushed the lead back to three for Carolina.

Roth's night ended with this line: 7⅔ innings, five hits, two earned runs, two walks and six strikeouts. On short rest, the left-hander threw 127 pitches. "Michael's got the biggest heart I've ever seen on a field," Walker said after the game. "He put us on his back today."

Facing the best hitters in the game, Roth finished his two-year run at the College World Series with a 1.17 earned-run average in 38⅓ innings. That was the second lowest in the event's history. Who knows? Maybe he will get a chance to lower it in 2012.

Roth's final ERA in 2011 was 1.06, the best in the nation. He won fourteen games and lost three. He had been special in 2010, but there was no fair value to put on Roth in 2011. His contributions were unmatched. He was a true ace on the field and a true captain off it. "As a coach," Tanner said, "you can't draw it up any better than the kind of influence he's had. It's hard to believe he's real sometimes."

The second championship was coming into focus for Carolina. Taylor allowed an inherited run in the eighth to score before handing the ball to Price with a 4–2 lead. The best closer in the country needed four outs. Price ended the top of the eighth by striking out Thompson.

Wingo singled in a run in the eighth to make the score 5–2, giving Price even more of a cushion. But Price, who had pitched in each of Carolina's five College World Series games, was running on his patented adrenaline. Insurance was not necessary. He could see the finish line, and it looked similar to the one in 2010.

Price needed three outs.

Johnson flied out to start the ninth. That was one.

Pinch hitter Jeff Moyer grounded to Walker at first. He stepped on the bag. That was two.

Another pinch hitter, Ben McMahan, then hit the second pitch he saw from Price into Bradley's glove in center field.

That was three outs. That was it. South Carolina would remain college baseball's national champion for another year. The school had waited a century for its first title of substance. The wait for the second was significantly shorter.

The heart of the team was on display in the victory. Roth had thrown a season high in pitches on three days' rest. Wingo had driven in a pair of runs. Injuries were supposed to knock Bradley and Walker from the College World Series, but they recorded every out in the ninth inning of the final game.

Even to the end, Carolina claimed it was the scrappy underdog. "We joked about being underrated and no one giving us any credit," Walker said. "I think we enjoyed that. We liked having that on our side. We thought, 'That's fine. We'll go out and show them. We'll make you think South Carolina should have been ranked number one.'"

The Gamecocks did just that. They did not start either 2010 or 2011 as the number one team in the country, but that's where they finished.

Reigning Champions

The team again celebrated with the customary dog pile, the players excitedly slamming into one another just in front of the mound at TD Ameritrade Park.

Charlie Peters had seen it form from the Rosenblatt stands in 2010. The team's good luck charm of a batboy wanted to take part in the newest dog pile. He was not quite sure how he fit in, however, since he was all of about five feet tall and weighed, oh, seventy-five pounds or so. "I didn't want to get smashed," he said.

Peters stood to the side, smiling and laughing hysterically, as he tried to plot his entrance into the mass. Finally, he just went for it. He stuck the landing and joined the party. "It was awesome," he said. "I was sitting on top of Evan Marzilli's head."

A year earlier, the Gamecocks had played—and won—for seven-year-old Bayler Teal, who lost his fight with cancer during the College World Series. Bayler's life and death connoted a lot of strong, serious and varied emotions. Thinking about his playful spirit, his maturity for a kid, immediately evoked a smile. But to see him pass away so young, with his whole life in front of him, was sad in an unspeakable way. To see two young parents grieve—along with Bayler's five-year-old brother, Bridges—was one of life's great injustices.

Bigger than the pain, though, Bayler inspired. He pushed Carolina's players, coaches and staff to greatness on the sport's biggest stage. He's still inspiring today. His legacy of joy through adversity will live forever.

Charlie's story was and is important because he is present. You can see him, talk to him, view the scars from his struggle in 2003. He has been to the edge and back. He knows those steps. So do his parents, Jenny and Matt, and their eight other children. (She had number nine, Ezekiel, in September 2011. She joked she has enough kids to field her own baseball team.)

To scores of people, including the Gamecocks, Charlie symbolizes hope. It's the platform on which the large south Omaha family has built their lives, having endured and defeated childhood cancer two different times with Morgan and Charlie. "We're living, breathing, happy examples of hope," Matt said. "This is what happens when you believe good things are possible, even when you're dealt a bad hand."

The first survivor in the family, twenty-year-old Morgan, has vowed to become a nurse. Charlie is still a bit young to decide his future plans, but it's a wonder to see him play and talk about baseball. He's a busy kid with a big spirit about him. The thirteen-year-old's potential is limitless. He had cancer. But you'd have no idea.

He connected to a college baseball team nearly a decade earlier. The cast of characters had changed a few times by its return in 2010, but the core of the team—what it stood for, instilled by Tanner—had not shifted at all. That's why players like Jackie Bradley Jr. and Michael Roth, generations removed from those in 2003, embraced Charlie the same way those such as Wade Jordan did. "I never thought it would turn into anything like it has," Jordan said.

Charlie didn't, either. He did not know if Tanner would remember him when the Gamecocks came back to Omaha in 2010. Tanner sure did—so much that he made him part of the team in 2011. "It means the world to me that a college baseball team remembers a sick five-year-old boy that they met in the hospital," Jenny said. "It means the world to me that they stuck with him for eight-plus years."

Hope has no boundaries. It is not confined by distance or time. It's omnipresent, if only it is acknowledged.

During the 2011 College World Series, the Gamecocks went back to Children's Hospital for another visit. Charlie and his family went, too. Tanner said that "it was like walking around with Elvis." Forget the players; Charlie was the celebrity because he had walked out of the hospital doors. He was living the life he wanted, setting the example for future survivors.

"That was as good as it gets," Tanner said. "I'm sitting there thinking, 'I hope that I can be like he is, with his resiliency and the courage that he has.' I admire Charlie Peters."

After the chaos of the victory had settled to some extent at TD Ameritrade Park, Scott Wingo was handed a trophy. He was the College World Series' Most Outstanding Player.

A guy who had lost his starting job on a couple of occasions, a .226 hitter his first three seasons, was the sport's biggest event's best player. Wingo had six hits and drove in four runs in the series, plus he contributed on most of South Carolina's nine double plays in its five College World Series games.

Wingo's season did not surprise his teammates, but it did bring all of them happiness to see what he had done. He was not drafted out of high school or after his junior season. But his offensive breakout in 2011 caught the Los Angeles Dodgers' eyes. They selected him in the eleventh round, still very early in the draft.

"People ask me all the time, 'Does Wingo have a chance to play for the Dodgers?'" Tanner said. "I say, 'You know what, I'm not sure. But I wouldn't bet against him.' The numbers are against you to get to the Big Leagues. It's staggering, actually. But he's not a guy I would doubt."

Before the NCAA Tournament began, a couple of reporters asked Wingo what he would like for his legacy to be at South Carolina. He thought for a few seconds before he answered. It meant something to Wingo, how he would be remembered. "A player that would pretty much do anything to win," he said. "Just get after it. Just get dirty. Somebody that they know is going to give it their all for them and play hard every game."

Wingo did that and more. He had already scored the title-winning run in 2010, so his place in South Carolina baseball history was assured. But in 2011 he became many fans' favorite Gamecock of all time. He got dirt on his uniform and played as hard as he always had, but Wingo had four game-winning hits and batted .338, second only to Christian Walker's .358.

He had gone from being a great defensive player to being a great player. And he was holding a trophy that signified he was the College World Series' Most Outstanding Player.

Interestingly enough, Wingo had called his shot. As the team left Carolina Stadium for Omaha, Wingo found his mom. "We're going to go back to back," he told Nancy Wingo. "We're going to win this thing again. We're not going out there to fool around."

He continued. "Momma, I'm going to win the MVP award, just for you." He boarded the bus and went to Omaha, and all of those things came true.

The team returned to Columbia to the same fanfare it had in 2010. There were again about fifteen thousand fans inside Colonial Life Arena for a day-after celebration. Just as they had the year before, the Gamecocks again paraded down Main Street to begin the Fourth of July weekend.

"This must be heaven!" Tanner shouted to begin the pep rally at the State House steps. The university's flag again was flying atop the capitol, along with the American and state flags.

The school's president, Harris Pastides, noted the shifting attitude at Carolina. The wait was over in 2010. The wait was short after 2010. "It used to be, 'Wait 'til next year,'" Pastides said. "Now it's, 'Let's do it again next year.'"

The players soon scattered after the parade, many of the draftees going to join their professional teams.

Wingo enjoyed "Scott Wingo Day" in his hometown of Mauldin before he left for Arizona to start climbing the Dodgers' minor-league ladder. "I was just hoping to go somewhere," Wingo said. "I didn't know where or when or what round." Two other seniors, John Taylor (Seattle, twenty-second round) and Adrian Morales (Kansas City, forty-ninth), headed out, too.

Peter Mooney (Toronto, twenty-first), Bryan Harper (Washington, thirtieth) and Steven Neff (San Francisco, forty-first) made relatively quick decisions to leave early. A few others, players who would be important pieces in 2012, took some time to think about it.

Jackie Bradley Jr. was taken fortieth overall in the sandwich round—the compensatory picks between the first and second rounds—by the Boston Red Sox. Matt Price was selected in the sixth round by Arizona. Adam Matthews went in the twenty-third round to Baltimore. Cleveland took Michael Roth in the thirty-first round.

Bradley insisted he would entertain coming back for his senior year, but a big part of that statement was leveraging. He signed with the Red Sox just before the August deadline. Price went back and forth but decided to return. He is expected to be a starter in 2012, though the door will always be open for him to again resume the role as closer. Matthews considered his options but ultimately decided he would like to erase the frustration of his injury-filled season in 2011—even with the titles and contributions in the College World Series.

And then there was Roth, who was forced to skip the parade—because he had to catch a flight to Spain. Roth had scheduled all along to spend a month abroad as part of his international business program. He had to adjust his schedule a little since the Gamecocks again stayed the maximum amount of time in Omaha.

Roth received a call from an Indians scout just before he left. He politely told him he would listen to what the club had to say but not until after he got back from Spain. Really, he did not seem to care much about professional baseball. That did not change much after he got back from Europe. Roth told the Indians thanks, but no thanks. He wanted to earn his degree and then worry about pro baseball.

Matthews, Price and Roth figured to provide a solid nucleus in 2012, along with Walker and the young pitchers such as Forrest Koumas and Colby Holmes. And winning national championships had not hurt the Gamecocks' ability to fare well on the recruiting trail.

Talk of a three-peat—somewhat serious, somewhat joking—had started before even the beginning of the 2012 season. Then again, it was instigated back in the summertime.

"Everything about it was perfect," Walker said just after winning the second title. "Maybe we can do it again next year."

The Gamecocks called themselves grinders, battlers, underdogs. But more than that, they were winners. They were champions. Again.

Yearbook

FEBRUARY 18
GAMECOCKS 12, SANTA CLARA 5
Team: 1-0
Win: Michael Roth (1-0)—5⅔ innings, 4 hits, 2 earned runs, walk, 6 strikeouts
Offensive star: CF Jackie Bradley Jr.—4 for 4, home run, 3 runs batted in
They said: "Even the great ones in this game make outs and he did not make an out today."—Coach Ray Tanner on Bradley

FEBRUARY 19
GAMECOCKS 2, SANTA CLARA 1
Team: 2-0
Win: Tyler Webb (1-0)—6 innings, 3 hits, 1 run, 2 walks, 4 strikeouts
Save: Matt Price (1)—1⅓ IP
Offensive star: 1B Christian Walker: 2 for 4
They said: "We're happy to win close games."—Tanner on first of thirteen one-run wins for Gamecocks

FEBRUARY 20
GAMECOCKS 6, SANTA CLARA 0
Team: 3-0
Win: Jose Mata (1-0)—⅔ inning, 1 hit, 1 walk
Offensive star: Walker—2 for 4, home run, 3 runs batted in
They said: "I'm seeing it pretty well."—Walker on going eight for twelve in first weekend series

FEBRUARY 25
GAMECOCKS 10, SOUTHERN ILLINOIS 6
Team: 4-0
Win: Roth (2-0)—6⅔ innings, 4 hits, 2 runs (1 earned), 2 walks, 9 strikeouts
Save: Price (2)—⅔ inning, 1 strikeout
Offensive star: C Brady Thomas—3 for 4, 2 doubles, 2 runs batted in
They said: "Coach is always in our ear about being aggressive with some of these pitchers."—catcher Robert Beary, who hit his first home run of the year

FEBRUARY 26
GAMECOCKS 4, SOUTHERN ILLINOIS 0
Team: 5-0
Win: Webb (2-0)—7⅓ innings, 4 hits, 1 walk, 7 strikeouts
Offensive star: RF Adam Matthews—2 for 4
They said: "He put himself in position to start and it looks like he wants to stay there."—Tanner on Webb

FEBRUARY 27
GAMECOCKS 9, SOUTHERN ILLINOIS 4
Team: 6-0
Win: John Taylor (1-0)—2⅔ innings, 1 hit, 5 strikeouts
Offensive star: 3B Adrian Morales—3 for 4, home run, 3 runs batted in
They said: "He is a guy, for me, that if I have two outs, I like to see him coming up there to the plate—especially in big situations."—Tanner on Morales

MARCH 1
GAMECOCKS 14, FURMAN 1
Team: 7-0
Win: Steven Neff (1-0)—4 innings, 2 hits, 1 walk, 7 strikeouts
Offensive star: Walker—2 for 3, home run, 4 runs batted in
They said: "We believe in him."—Tanner on Neff

MARCH 4
GAMECOCKS 6, CLEMSON 3
Team: 8-0
Win: Roth (3-0)—7 innings, 7 hits, 3 runs (0 earned), 3 walks, 6 strikeouts
Save: Price (3)—1⅓ innings, 3 strikeouts
Offensive star: Walker—2 for 3, home run, 2 runs batted in
They said: "I didn't expect it. Brady got us back in it and Walker hit his a long way."—Tanner on erasing an early 3–0 deficit with homers from Thomas and Walker

MARCH 6
CLEMSON 10, GAMECOCKS 5
In Clemson
Team: 8-1
Loss: Price (0-1)—⅔ inning, 4 hits, 6 earned runs, 2 walks
Offensive star—Walker: 2 for 4, home run, run batted in

MARCH 8
GAMECOCKS 5, CLEMSON 4
In Greenville
Team: 9-1
Win: Forrest Koumas (1-0)—2⅓ innings, 3 hits, 3 earned runs, 1 walk, 3 strikeouts
Save: Price (4)—1 inning, 1 hit, 1 strikeout
Offensive star: PH Jake Williams—1 for 1, home run, 3 runs batted in

MARCH 11
GAMECOCKS 5, CAL STATE–BAKERSFIELD 1
Team: 10-1
Win: Roth (4-0)—8 innings, 5 hits, 1 run (0 earned), 1 walk, 9 strikeouts
Offensive star: Bradley—3 for 3, home run, 3 runs batted in
They said: "He's been outstanding. He's done everything he can do as a starter."—Tanner on Roth

MARCH 12
GAMECOCKS 5, CAL STATE–BAKERSFIELD 2
Team: 11-1
Win: Neff (2-0)—5⅓ innings, 4 hits, 1 earned run, 2 strikeouts
Offensive star: Beary—2 for 2
They said: "I think it gives you a feel that it could be a 'new bat era' game."—Tanner on each of the team's nine hits being singles

MARCH 13
CAL STATE–BAKERSFIELD 8, GAMECOCKS 3
Team: 11-2
Loss: Webb (2-1)—2⅓ innings, 3 hits, 4 runs (2 earned), 4 walks, 2 strikeouts
Offensive star: Walker—2 for 4, 2 doubles
They said: "I didn't throw enough strikes today."—Webb

MARCH 15
FURMAN 4, GAMECOCKS 2
In Greenville
Team: 11-3
Loss: Westmoreland (0-1)—2 innings, 4 hits, 2 earned runs, 2 walks
Offensive star: Morales—2 for 4, run batted in.

MARCH 16
GAMECOCKS 8, WOFFORD 4
Team: 12-3
Win: Colby Holmes (1-0)—5⅓ innings, 1 hit, 2 earned runs, 3 walks, 4 strikeouts
Offensive star: Morales—3 for 3, home run, run batted in.
They said: "There was urgency, for me. We play fifty-six regular-season games, and they are all important."—Tanner on losing two in a row entering Wofford game

MARCH 18
GEORGIA 4, GAMECOCKS 2
Team: 12-4, 0-1 SEC
Win: Roth (4-1)—6⅓ innings, 6 hits, 3 runs (2 earned), 2 walks, 8 strikeouts
Offensive star: Thomas—2 for 4, home run, run batted in
They said: "We didn't play as well as you could like to, of course."—Tanner on the team committing five errors

MARCH 19
GAMECOCKS 2, GEORGIA 1
Team: 13-4, 1-1 SEC
Win: Price (1-1)—1 inning, 2 hits, 2 strikeouts
Offensive star: Morales—3 for 4
They said: "We came out today with fight and focus. We were ready to go."—Scott Wingo, who had the game-winning infield single in the ninth

MARCH 20
GAMECOCKS 8, GEORGIA 3
Team: 14-4, 2-1 SEC
Win: Koumas (2-0)—3⅓ innings, 2 hits, 1 earned run, 3 walks, 6 strikeouts
Save: Price (5)—2 innings, 1 hit, 4 strikeouts
Offensive star: Matthews—3 for 3, run batted in
They said: "This team, we fight hard. We show up together every day."—Morales on team rallying to win series after Friday loss

MARCH 22
GAMECOCKS 24, COLLEGE OF CHARLESTON 4
Team: 15-4
Win: Holmes (2-0)—6 innings, 5 hits, 3 earned runs, 2 walks, 6 strikeouts
Offensive star: Matthews—3 for 6, 2 home runs, double, 8 runs batted in
They said: "Tonight, Adam was fantastic."—Tanner on Matthews

MARCH 23
GAMECOCKS 17, RHODE ISLAND 8
Team: 16-4
Win: Mata (2-0)—4 innings, 2 hits, 1 earned run, 2 strikeouts
Offensive star: Beary—4 for 6, home run, 4 runs batted in
They said: "I have been extremely happy with what we have been able to do
    offensively early in the game in the last four, five, six games."—Tanner on
    team, which had scored forty-one runs in two nights

MARCH 25
GAMECOCKS 9, FLORIDA 2
In Gainesville, Florida
Team: 17-4, 3-1 SEC
Win: Roth (5-1)—8⅓ innings, 10 hits, 2 earned runs, 2 walks, 6 strikeouts
Offensive star: Williams—3 for 5, home run, run batted in

MARCH 26
FLORIDA 2, GAMECOCKS 1
In Gainesville, Florida
Team: 17-5, 3-2 SEC
Loss: Price (1-2)—2 innings, 1 hit, 1 earned run, 2 walks, 3 strikeouts
Offensive star: Bradley—2 for 4

MARCH 27
GAMECOCKS 4, FLORIDA 3
In Gainesville, Florida
Team: 18-5, 4-2 SEC
Win: Price (2-2)—2⅓ innings, 1 hit, 1 strikeout
Offensive star: Matthews—2 for 4, double

MARCH 30
GAMECOCKS 6, THE CITADEL 4
Team: 19-5
Win: Taylor (2-0)—2 innings, 1 walk, 3 strikeouts
Save: Price (6)—1 inning, 2 strikeouts

Offensive star: Walker—2 for 4, home run, 4 runs batted in

They said: "It was the key to the game."—Tanner on six scoreless innings from the team's bullpen

APRIL 1
GAMECOCKS 3, KENTUCKY 1

Team: 20-5, 5-2 SEC

Win: Roth (6-1)—8 innings, 3 hits, 1 earned run, 1 walk, 6 strikeouts

Save: Price (7)—1 inning, 1 hit

Offensive star: SS Peter Mooney—1 for 2, home run, run batted in

They said: "Roth battled, we played good defense and we were able to make some plays."—Tanner

APRIL 2
GAMECOCKS 4, KENTUCKY 3 (10 INNINGS)

Team: 21-5, 6-2 SEC

Win: Price (3-2)—2 innings, 2 strikeouts

Offensive star: Thomas—3 for 5, double, 2 runs batted in

They said: "He has a reputation of being that kind of guy. He seems to have his better at-bats when the chips are down."—Tanner on Thomas's game-winning hit in the tenth inning

APRIL 3
GAMECOCKS 4, KENTUCKY 1

Team: 22-5, 7-2 SEC

Win: Koumas (3-0)—6⅓ innings, 2 hits, 1 walk, 3 strikeouts

Offensive star: Mooney—3 for 3

They said: "Very, very happy to win all three games this weekend. That doesn't happen much in this conference."—Tanner on the first of three SEC sweeps for the team

APRIL 5
GAMECOCKS 18, USC–UPSTATE 2

Team: 23-5

Win: Patrick Sullivan (1-0)—5 innings, 2 hits, 1 earned run, 2 walks, 6 strikeouts

Offensive star: Walker—5 for 6, home run, double, 5 runs batted in

They said: "I just tried to play my game and get a couple of hits."—Walker

APRIL 7
GAMECOCKS 4, TENNESSEE 0
In Knoxville, Tennessee
Team: 24-5, 8-2 SEC
Win: Roth (7-1)—7⅔ innings, 6 hits, 1 walk, 4 strikeouts
Save: Price (8)—1⅓ innings, 1 hit, 1 walk, 1 strikeout
Offensive star: Wingo—3 for 4

APRIL 8
GAMECOCKS 2, TENNESSEE 0
In Knoxville, Tennessee
Team: 25-5, 9-2 SEC
Win: Holmes (3-0)—7 innings, 3 hits, 7 strikeouts
Save: Price (9)—⅓ inning, 1 strikeout
Offensive star: Walker—1 for 4, home run, 2 runs batted in

APRIL 9
GAMECOCKS 2, TENNESSEE 1
In Knoxville, Tennessee
Team: 26-5, 10-2 SEC
Win: Koumas (4-0)—7⅓ innings, 3 hits, 1 earned run, 2 walks, 7 strikeouts
Save: Price (10)—1⅓ innings, 2 hits, 1 walk, 2 strikeouts
Offensive star: Wingo—2 for 3

APRIL 12
THE CITADEL 2, GAMECOCKS 0
In Charleston
Team: 26-6
Loss: Neff (2-1)—3⅓ innings, 2 hits, 2 earned runs, 1 walk
Offensive star: Thomas—4 for 4

APRIL 15
GAMECOCKS 3, VANDERBILT 1
Team: 27-6, 11-2 SEC
Win: Roth (8-1)—7⅔ innings, 3 hits, 1 earned run, 2 walks, 8 strikeouts
Save: Price (11)—1⅓ innings, 4 strikeouts
Offensive star: Wingo—2 for 3
They said: "Facing Sonny Gray tonight we all had our hands full, and he kept us in position to win."—Tanner on Roth outdueling the future first-rounder

APRIL 16
VANDERBILT 6, GAMECOCKS 4
Team: 27-7, 11-3 SEC
Loss: Holmes (3-1)—4⅓ innings, 7 hits, 6 earned runs, 1 walk, 4 strikeouts
Offensive star: Thomas—2 for 3, home run, 2 runs batted in
They said: "We won a close one last night and lost a close one tonight. They have outstanding players and great pitchers."—Tanner on Vanderbilt, ranked No. 1 entering the series

APRIL 17
GAMECOCKS 5, VANDERBILT 3
Team: 28-7, 12-3 SEC
Win: Price (4-2)—3 innings, 2 hits, 7 strikeouts
Offensive star: Wingo—1 for 3, double, 2 runs batted in
They said: "I started taking batting practice on Wednesday, and I was seeing the ball good today. I hit in high school, so it's really nothing new."—pitcher Steven Neff, who was thrust into the lineup due to injuries and doubled in the team's four-run seventh inning

APRIL 19
GAMECOCKS 8, COLLEGE OF CHARLESTON 3
In Mount Pleasant
Team: 29-7
Win: Bryan Harper (1-0)—2⅓ innings, 4 walks, 3 strikeouts
Offensive star: Beary—2 for 5, 2 runs batted in

APRIL 22
GAMECOCKS 8, MISSISSIPPI STATE 2
In Starkville, Mississippi
Team: 30-7, 13-3 SEC
Win: Roth (9-1)—6⅓ innings, 3 hits, 2 runs (1 earned), 3 walks, 4 strikeouts
Offensive star: Walker—4 for 5

APRIL 23
MISSISSIPPI STATE 5, GAMECOCKS 3
In Starkville, Mississippi
Team: 30-8, 13-4 SEC
Loss: Taylor (2-1)—⅓ inning, 2 hits, 2 runs (1 earned)
Offensive star: Beary—1 for 2, 2 runs batted in

APRIL 24
GAMECOCKS 13, MISSISSIPPI STATE 4
In Starkville, Mississippi
Team: 31-8, 14-4 SEC
Win: Taylor (3-1)—4 innings, 4 hits, 1 earned run, 1 walk, 3 strikeouts
Offensive star: Walker—4 for 4, home run, double, 4 runs batted in
They said: "We didn't have a more satisfying win."—associate head coach
    Chad Holbrook on team winning day after losing Bradley to a broken wrist

APRIL 26
GAMECOCKS 9, LIBERTY 6
Team: 32-8
Win: Mata (3-0)—2 innings, 1 hit, 2 earned runs, 2 walks, 1 strikeout
Save: Price (12)—1 inning, 2 strikeouts
Offensive star: Roth—1 for 2, 2 runs batted in
They said: "Coach Tanner said stay ready for an opportunity to pinch
    hit."—Roth, the team's ace, on his RBI hit

APRIL 29
GAMECOCKS 2, AUBURN 1
Team: 33-8, 15-4 SEC
Win: Taylor (4-1)—1 inning
Offensive star: Wingo—1 for 5, run batted in
They said: "I was thinking at this last at-bat, here, 'I've got to give it my all,' and
    it turned out well."—Wingo on his game-winning single in the ninth inning

APRIL 30
GAMECOCKS 10, AUBURN 2
Team: 34-8, 16-4 SEC
Win: Holmes (4-1)—7⅓ innings, 4 hits, 2 earned runs, 3 walks, 7 strikeouts
Offensive star: CF Evan Marzilli—2 for 3, 2 runs batted in
They said: "We started to catch fire, and everyone had the bat hot a little
    bit."—Marzilli on the team's six-run seventh inning

MAY 1
GAMECOCKS 7, AUBURN 3
Team: 35-8, 17-4 SEC
Win: Koumas (5-0)—5 innings, 4 hits, 2 earned runs, 2 walks, 3 strikeouts
Save: Price (13)—2 innings, 1 hit, 2 walks, 2 strikeouts
Offensive star: Morales—3 for 5, run batted in
They said: "We control our destiny. We've got to continue to play well and
    not look at the standings."—Morales

MAY 4
GAMECOCKS 9, WOFFORD 3
In Spartanburg
Team: 36-8
Win: Westmoreland (1-1)—5⅓ innings, 6 hits, 2 earned runs, 4 walks, 5 strikeouts
Offensive star: Walker—4 for 5, double, run batted in

MAY 6
GAMECOCKS 6, MISSISSIPPI 1
In Oxford, Mississippi
Team: 37-8, 18-4 SEC
Win: Roth (10-1)—8 innings, 6 hits, 1 earned run, 1 walk, 6 strikeouts
Offensive star: Beary—3 for 4, run batted in

MAY 7
MISSISSIPPI 10, GAMECOCKS 2
In Oxford, Mississippi
Team: 37-9, 18-5 SEC
Loss: Holmes (4-2)—1⅓ innings, 4 hits, 3 earned runs, 1 walk, 2 strikeouts
Offensive star: Marzilli—2 for 3, run batted in

MAY 8
MISSISSIPPI 7, GAMECOCKS 6
In Oxford, Mississippi
Team: 37-10, 18-6 SEC
Loss: Price (4-3)—3 innings, 2 hits, 1 earned run, 2 walks, 1 strikeout
Offensive star: Thomas—2 for 4, triple, double, 2 runs batted in

MAY 10
GAMECOCKS 6, PRESBYTERIAN 1
Team: 38-10
Win: Neff (3-1)—5 innings, 5 hits, 1 earned run, 1 walk, 5 strikeouts
Offensive star: Mooney—2 for 4, home run, 2 runs batted in
They said: "He gave us five innings, and I was happy with his outing."—Tanner on Neff, who had been playing in the outfield and ran into a fence at Ole Miss two days before making the start against the Blue Hose

MAY 11
GAMECOCKS 11, CHARLESTON SOUTHERN 1
Team: 39-10
Win: Sullivan (2-0)—6 innings, 6 hits, 1 earned run, 1 walk, 6 strikeouts
Offensive star: Mooney—2 for 5, 2 doubles, 3 runs batted in
They said: "If we score eleven every time out, we can find a way to win."—Mooney

MAY 13
ARKANSAS 6, GAMECOCKS 2
Team: 39-11, 18-7 SEC
Loss: Roth (10-2)—5⅓ innings, 10 hits, 3 runs (2 earned), 1 walk, 5 strikeouts
Offensive star: DH DeSean Anderson—2 for 3, double, run batted in
They said: "They did a good job of swinging the bat. No doubt about it."—
   Tanner on Arkansas, which rocked the Gamecocks for fourteen hits

MAY 14
GAMECOCKS 6, ARKANSAS 5
Team: 40-11, 19-7 SEC
Win: Price (5-3)—2⅓ innings, 2 hits, 2 earned runs, 2 walks, 4 strikeouts
Offensive star: Neff—3 for 4, home run, double, 2 runs batted in
They said: "We knew we needed a win today."—Wingo, who blasted a walk-
   off home run in the ninth inning to save the series

MAY 15
GAMECOCKS 7, ARKANSAS 1
Team: 41-11, 20-7 SEC
Win: Holmes (5-2)—8⅔ innings, 6 hits, 1 earned run, 1 walk, 7 strikeouts
Offensive star: Neff—3 for 4, 2 home runs, 3 runs batted in
They said: "The more at-bats I get, the more I get to see the ball."—Neff on
   hitting three home runs in two games against Arkansas

MAY 17
GAMECOCKS 9, UNC–ASHEVILLE 5
Team: 42-11
Win: Webb (3-1)—2 innings, 2 hits, 3 runs (0 earned), 2 walks, 3 strikeouts
Save: Mata (1)—2⅓ innings, 3 hits, 2 strikeouts
Offensive star: Williams—4 for 5, double, 4 runs batted in
They said: "The more at-bats I get, the more I get to see the ball."—Neff on
   hitting three home runs in two games against Arkansas

MAY 19
ALABAMA 2, GAMECOCKS 1
In Tuscaloosa, Alabama
Team: 42-12, 20-8 SEC
Loss: Roth (10-3)—9 innings, 5 hits, 1 run (0 earned), 3 walks, 5 strikeouts
Offensive star: Walker—2 for 4, run batted in

MAY 20
GAMECOCKS 6, ALABAMA 3
In Tuscaloosa, Alabama
Team: 43-12, 21-8 SEC
Win: Koumas (6-0)—5 innings, 5 hits, 1 earned run, 5 strikeouts
Save: Price (14)—3 innings, 5 hits, 2 earned runs, 4 strikeouts
Offensive star: Marzilli—3 for 4, double, 2 runs batted in

MAY 21
GAMECOCKS 3, ALABAMA 2
In Tuscaloosa, Alabama
Team: 44-12, 22-8 SEC
Win: Holmes (6-2)—6⅔ innings, 4 hits, 1 earned run, 4 walks, 5 strikeouts
Save: Price (15)—1⅓ innings, 2 strikeouts
Offensive star: Marzilli—4 for 4, 2 doubles

MAY 25
GAMECOCKS 7, AUBURN 3
In Hoover, Alabama—SEC Tournament
Team: 45-12
Win: Roth (11-3)—9 innings, 6 hits, 3 runs (0 earned), 2 walks, 2 strikeouts
Offensive star: Marzilli—2 for 2, double, 2 runs batted in
They said: "The day didn't start out so well…but I'm proud of all these guys hanging in there and really coming away with a good victory today. Michael pitched extremely well for the final eight innings."—Tanner on team overcoming Auburn's three-run first inning

MAY 26
VANDERBILT 7, GAMECOCKS 2
In Hoover, Alabama—SEC Tournament
Team: 45-13
Loss: Koumas (6-1)—4⅓ innings, 4 hits, 3 runs (2 earned), 4 walks, 3 strikeouts
Offensive star: Walker—3 for 4
They said: "They had the best pitcher, Sonny Gray, out there, and he gave us some tough pitches."—Morales

MAY 27
GEORGIA 4, GAMECOCKS 2
In Hoover, Alabama—SEC Tournament
Team: 45-14
Loss: Holmes (6-3)—5 innings, 6 hits, 4 runs (3 earned), 1 walk, 5 strikeouts
Offensive star: Marzilli—2 for 4, 2 runs batted in
They said: "I think we'll be fine at home. We'll just have to see who is in our regional and come out and beat them like we've been doing all year."—Morales

JUNE 3
GAMECOCKS 2, GEORGIA SOUTHERN 1
NCAA Regional
Team: 46-14
Win: Roth (12-3)—7 innings, 2 hits, 1 run (0 earned), 2 walks, 4 strikeouts
Save: Price (16)—1⅔ innings, 3 strikeouts
Offensive star: Thomas—1 for 3, run batted in
They said: "When you have guys like that, that have been in situations many, many times, you feel good about what's going to happen."—Tanner on Roth and Price's pitching all but one out of a close, low-scoring game

JUNE 4
GAMECOCKS 11, STETSON 5
NCAA Regional
Team: 47-14
Win: Holmes (7-3)—6⅔ innings, 7 hits, 4 earned runs, 1 walk, 3 strikeouts
Offensive star: Beary—2 for 3, home run, double, 4 runs batted in
They said: "Guys up and down the order all can swing it. That's how we got in the position we're in now."—Marzilli on the bottom-of-the-lineup production

JUNE 5
GAMECOCKS 8, STETSON 2
NCAA Regional
Team: 48-14
Win: Taylor (5-1)—1⅔ innings, 2 hits, 1 earned run, 2 walks
Save: Price (17)—2⅔ innings, 2 hits, 2 strikeouts
Offensive star: Beary—2 for 5, triple, run batted in
They said: "I mean it's big, but at the same time we're just trying to win and keep winning, trying to get to that main goal at the end."—Price on advancing to the super regional

JUNE 11
GAMECOCKS 5, CONNECTICUT 1
NCAA Super Regional
Team: 49-14
Win: Roth (13-3)—8⅓ innings, 6 hits, 1 run (0 earned), 3 walks, 2 strikeouts
Offensive star: Wingo—2 for 5, 2 runs batted in
They said: "I thought the team that played better won the ballgame. South Carolina played better than we did and deserved to win the ballgame."—UConn coach Jim Penders

JUNE 12
GAMECOCKS 8, CONNECTICUT 2
NCAA Super Regional
Team: 50-14
Win: Taylor (6-1)—1⅔ innings, 2 hits, 1 walk, 1 strikeout
Save: Price (18)—2 innings, 2 hits, 1 walk, 4 strikeouts
Offensive star: Walker—1 for 4, home run, run batted in
They said: "I enjoy situations like that."—Walker on the game-winning home run in the top of the eighth, which then led to a five-run ninth to break open the game and send the Gamecocks back to Omaha

JUNE 19
GAMECOCKS 5, TEXAS A&M 4
Omaha, Nebraska—NCAA College World Series
Team: 51-14
Win: Price (6-3)—⅔ inning, 1 strikeout
Offensive star: Wingo—4 for 4, double, run batted in
They said: "We couldn't get him out."—Texas A&M coach Rob Childress on Wingo, who was on base five times and won the game with a ninth-inning single off the wall in right field

JUNE 21
GAMECOCKS 7, VIRGINIA 1
Omaha, Nebraska—NCAA College World Series
Team: 52-14
Win: Taylor (7-1)—4⅓ innings, 1 hit, 1 walk
Offensive star: Walker—2 for 5, double, 2 runs batted in
They said: "We probably can't play any better than that."—Tanner

JUNE 24
GAMECOCKS 3, VIRGINIA 2 (13 INNINGS)
Omaha, Nebraska—NCAA College World Series
Team: 53-14
Win: Price (7-3)—5⅔ innings, 7 hits, 5 walks, 5 strikeouts
Offensive star: Thomas—2 for 6, double, 2 runs batted in
They said: "South Carolina has something very, very special going on right
now."—Virginia coach Brian O'Connor

JUNE 27
GAMECOCKS 2, FLORIDA 1 (11 INNINGS)
Omaha, Nebraska—NCAA College World Series
Championship Series—Game 1
Team: 54-14
Win: Taylor (8-1)—2 innings, 3 hits, 3 walks
Save: Price (19)—1 inning, 1 hit, 1 strikeout
Offensive star: Walker—2 for 5, double
They said: "We keep fighting. We've done it all year. Hopefully we continue
to do so."—Walker, who excelled despite having a broken bone in his
left hand

JUNE 28
GAMECOCKS 5, FLORIDA 2
Omaha, Nebraska—NCAA College World Series
Championship Series—Game 2
Team: 55-14
Win: Roth (14-3)—7⅔ innings, 5 hits, 2 earned runs, 2 walks, 6 strikeouts
Save: Price (20)—1⅓ innings, 1 strikeout
Offensive star: Mooney—2 for 3, home run, run batted in
They said: "Everything about it was perfect."—Walker on South Carolina
winning all five of its College World Series games to claim the school's
second consecutive national championship

VIRGINIA	4
CALIFORNIA	1
GAME 3	

VIRGINIA 1

GAME 8

TEXAS A&M	4
SOUTH CAROLINA	5
GAME 4	

SOUTH CAROLINA 7

SOUTH
CAROLINA 3

GAME 12
(13 INN.)

GAME 10

CHAMPIONSH

SOUTH CAROLINA

FLORIDA

GAME
(11 INN

SOUTH CAROLINA

FLORIDA

GAME

GAME 7	
CALIFORNIA	7
TEXAS A&M	3

CALIFORNIA 1

VIRGINIA 8

VIRGINIA 2

WORLD SERIES BRACKET

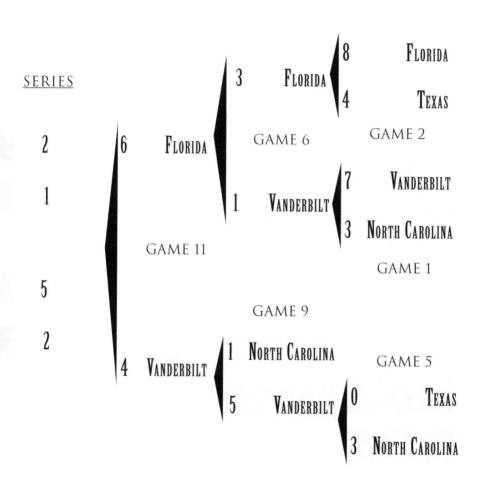

SERIES

2

1

5

2

6 FLORIDA

4 VANDERBILT

GAME 11

3 FLORIDA

1 VANDERBILT

GAME 6

1 NORTH CAROLINA

5 VANDERBILT

GAME 9

8 FLORIDA

4 TEXAS

GAME 2

7 VANDERBILT

3 NORTH CAROLINA

GAME 1

GAME 5

0 TEXAS

3 NORTH CAROLINA

2011 South Carolina Baseball Stats

GAMES SUMMARY

Score by innings	1	2	3	4	5	6	7	8	9	Ex.	Total
South Carolina	51	55	42	46	55	58	47	44	18	3	419
Opponents	32	29	25	15	14	24	22	32	19	0	212

2011 South Carolina Baseball Stats

Record When...

Overall	55-14
Conference	22-8
Non-conference	33-6
Home games	36-4
Away games	12-8
Neutral site	7-2
Day games	20-4
Night games	35-10
v. left starter	22-7
v. right starter	33-7
1-run games	13-3
2-run games	5-6
5+-run games	22-4
Extra innings	3-0
Shutouts	4-1

Scoring

0–2 runs	7-9
3–5 runs	16-4
6–9 runs	22-1
10+ runs	10-0

Opponent

0–2 runs	31-3
3–5 runs	21-4
6–9 runs	3-5
10+ runs	0-2

Scored in 1st inning	22-1
Opp. scored in 1st	12-8
Scores first	32-2
Opp. scores first	23-12

After 6

Leading	45-0
Trailing	4-13
Tied	6-1

After 7

Leading	48-1
Trailing	3-12
Tied	4-1

After 8

Leading	48-0
Trailing	0-13
Tied	7-1

Hit 0 home runs	27-11
1 home run	19-2
2+ home runs	9-1
Opponent 0 home runs	40-10
1 home run	9-2
2+ home runs	6-2

Made 0 errors	25-3
1 error	21-4
2+ errors	9-7
Opp. made 0 errors	17-5
1 error	20-8
2+ errors	18-1

Out-hit opponent	43-3
Out-hit by opponent	6-10
Hits are tied	6-1

Record When Team Scores

Runs	0	1	2	3	4	5	6	7	8	9	10+
W-L	0-1	0-2	7-6	4-2	5-1	7-1	7-1	4-0	6-0	5-0	10-0

Record When Opponent Scores

Runs	0	1	2	3	4	5	6	7	8	9	10+
W-L	4-0	17-0	10-3	10-0	7-3	4-1	2-2	0-2	1-1	0-0	0-2

Record When Leading After

Inning	1	2	3	4	5	6	7	8
W-L	18-1	25-3	31-1	37-1	39-1	45-0	48-1	48-0

Record When Trailing After

Inning	1	2	3	4	5	6	7	8
W-L	7-8	9-8	11-11	10-11	6-11	4-13	3-12	0-13

Record When Tied After

Inning	1	2	3	4	5	6	7	8
W-L	30-5	21-3	13-2	8-2	10-2	6-1	4-1	7-1

Current winning streak: 10
Longest winning streak: 10
Longest losing streak: 2

Home attendance: 297,279 (40 dates' average = 7,431)
Away attendance: 247,750 (29 dates' average = 8,543)
Total attendance: 545,029 (69 dates' average = 7,898)

Season Box Score

Record: 55-14   Home: 36-4   Away: 12-8   Neutral: 7-2   SEC: 22-8

Player	avg	gp-gs	ab	r	h	2b	3b	hr	rbi	tb
13 Christian Walker	.358	69-69	271	64	97	21	1	10	62	150
8 Scott Wingo	.338	69-68	240	47	81	8	1	4	31	103
36 Brady Thomas	.316	63-60	231	32	73	10	3	4	43	101
31 Evan Marzilli	.291	65-59	220	39	64	14	2	3	31	91
4 Robert Beary	.289	65-60	211	31	61	14	1	3	35	86
3 Adrian Morales	.281	68-68	249	44	70	16	0	3	40	95
6 Peter Mooney	.280	69-69	254	45	71	15	1	4	37	100
40 Jake Williams	.268	62-58	209	29	56	10	6	2	38	84
19 Jackie Bradley Jr.	.247	42-42	162	32	40	10	1	6	27	70

----

20 Jake Watson	.500	10-1	4	1	2	1	0	0	3	3
18 Dante Rosenberg	.500	2-1	2	0	1	0	0	0	1	1
34 Greg Brodzinski	.333	10-2	12	3	4	0	0	0	2	4
26 Adam Matthews	.264	34-29	110	26	29	4	2	2	14	43
9 Steven Neff	.254	23-18	71	11	18	7	0	5	7	40
30 Erik Payne	.250	9-2	8	2	2	1	0	0	0	3
29 Michael Roth	.200	11-3	15	3	3	1	0	0	4	4
42 DeSean Anderson	.191	21-13	47	10	9	4	0	0	5	13
5 Patrick Harrington	.000	3-1	3	0	0	0	0	0	0	0
22 Matt Price	.000	1-0	1	0	0	0	0	0	0	0
Totals	.294	69	2320	419	681	136	18	46	380	991
Opponents	.227	69	2250	212	511	70	4	28	192	673

LOB—Team (602), Opp (544). DPs turned—Team (81), Opp (38). CI—Team (1), Thomas 1, Opp (2). IBB—Team (16), Walker 6, Morales 3, Roth 2, Williams 2, Bradley Jr. 2, Beary 1, Opp (16). Picked off—Morales 2, Wingo 1, Matthews 1, Thomas 1, Walker 1.

slg%	bb	hp	so	gdp	ob%	sf	sh	sb-att	po	a	e	fld%
.554	36	6	30	6	.438	4	0	4-7	629	25	9	.986
.429	44	17	36	1	.467	3	10	7-8	137	245	11	.972
.437	23	2	46	5	.375	5	4	1-1	320	22	5	.986
.414	25	6	63	0	.375	2	10	6-7	115	6	3	.976
.408	12	10	26	5	.352	3	7	4-4	266	22	2	.993
.382	30	12	35	4	.378	5	4	7-11	38	129	11	.938
.394	44	5	31	2	.390	5	14	3-6	97	188	14	.953
.402	21	11	29	3	.361	3	7	1-4	79	1	0	1.000
.432	22	4	38	0	.346	3	1	2-3	86	2	2	.978
.750	1	0	1	0	.600	0	0	1-1	1	1	0	1.000
.500	0	0	0	0	.500	0	0	0-0	6	1	0	1.000
.333	0	2	1	0	.429	0	0	0-0	6	0	0	1.000
.391	16	2	22	0	.367	0	7	4-6	31	1	2	.941
.563	2	1	20	1	.284	0	1	0-0	16	6	2	.917
.375	0	0	2	0	.250	0	0	0-0	0	1	0	1.000
.267	4	0	5	1	.368	0	0	0-0	8	35	2	.956
.277	6	1	14	1	.291	1	4	1-1	8	0	0	1.000
.000	2	0	2	0	.400	0	0	0-0	0	0	0	.000
.000	0	0	1	0	.000	0	0	0-0	2	7	0	1.000
.427	288	79	402	29	.385	34	69	41-59	1859	747	69	.974
.299	228	71	53	63	.316	12	53	38-54	1771	637	72	.971

Player	era	w-l	app	gs	cg	sho	sv	ip	h
29 Michael Roth	1.06	14-3	21	20	1	0/1	0	145.0	108
14 John Taylor	1.14	8-1	50	0	0	0/2	0	71.1	45
27 Forrest Koumas	2.96	6-1	19	12	0	0/1	0	73.0	59
44 Colby Holmes	3.69	7-3	18	13	0	0/1	0	85.1	76
--------------------									
33 Alex Burrell	0.00	0-0	2	0	0	0/0	0	0.1	1
39 Patrick Sullivan	1.35	2-0	10	2	0	0/0	1	20.0	14
17 Jose Mata	1.76	3-0	23	0	0	0/1	1	30.2	30
22 Matt Price	1.83	7-3	36	0	0	0/2	20	59.0	44
9 Steven Neff	2.45	3-1	12	7	0	0/0	0	36.2	29
38 Tyler Webb	3.00	3-1	22	5	0	0/1	0	36.0	34
45 Bryan Harper	5.40	1-0	22	1	0	0/1	1	18.1	17
25 Adam Westmoreland	5.77	1-1	11	9	0	0/1	0	34.1	41
11 Will Casey	6.75	0-0	3	0	0	0/0	0	2.2	1
35 Logan Munson	7.71	0-0	11	0	0	0/1	0	7.0	12
Totals	2.45	55-14	69	69	1	4/4	23	619.2	511
Opponents	5.55	14-55	69	69	5	1/1	8	590.1	681

PB—Team (14), Thomas 7, Beary 5, Brodzinski 1, Rosenberg 1, Opp (15). Pickoffs—Team (3), Roth 3, Opp (6). SBA/ATT—Thomas (23-28), Beary (15-24), Koumas (7-12), Roth (7-11), Westmoreland (9-10), Mata (7-8), Holmes (3-5), Price (2-3), Taylor (2-2), Sullivan (0-1), Neff (0-1), Webb (1-1).

2011 South Carolina Baseball Stats

r	er	bb	so	2b	3b	hr	b/avg	wp	hp	bk	sfa	sha
36	17	41	112	16	2	3	.208	9	12	0	1	17
12	9	28	63	7	0	0	.185	2	9	2	1	6
28	24	29	63	7	1	3	.230	2	14	2	6	7
38	35	21	77	12	0	13	.232	4	6	1	0	2
0	0	0	0	1	0	0	.333	0	1	0	0	0
5	3	9	21	2	0	1	.203	1	0	0	1	1
7	6	13	16	4	0	0	.263	0	6	0	0	3
12	12	20	75	5	1	1	.213	2	7	0	1	5
11	10	10	29	3	0	0	.228	3	6	106		
19	12	17	28	8	0	1	.248	2	3	1	0	3
12	11	17	18	1	0	0	.250	5	0	0	0	3
23	22	18	26	3	0	5	.299	2	3	1	1	0
2	2	3	3	0	0	1	.111	0	0	0	0	0
7	6	2	5	1	0	0	.364	1	4	0	1	0
212	169	228	536	70	4	28	.227	33	71	8	12	53
419	364	288	402	136	18	46	.294	46	79	8	34	69

Chad Holbrook's Twitter Countdown

On New Year's Eve 2011, South Carolina associate head coach Chad Holbrook (@cholbrook2) compiled on Twitter his top ten moments from the Gamecocks' second championship season. Holbrook had gone on multiple occasions to the College World Series with his alma mater, North Carolina, but the Tar Heels never broke through. Now he's won two in a row with South Carolina.

10. Facing the possibility of starting the SEC regular season 0-2, @ScottWingo8 delivers a walk-off infield single to beat Georgia.

9. @mtRoth [Michael Roth] outdueling first-round pick Alex Meyer to help us beat Kentucky on Friday night. That set the tone for the whole weekend.

8. Game 3 vs. Vandy on a Sunday afternoon in Carolina Stadium. Could not have been a better college baseball atmosphere. @MattPrice22 shut it down.

7. Game 3 in Gainesville against No. 1 Florida. An absolutely huge accomplishment to win that road series against an incredibly talented team.

6. (tie) For lots of reasons, Sunday's game at Mississippi State was our most satisfying regular-season win. Coach Tanner teared up. He was that proud!

6. (tie) Friday night vs. Clemson. Crazy atmosphere. And @BradyThomas36 got us going with a big home run. Winning that series was special.

5. @CWALK01313's [Christian Walker] HR vs. UConn [in the super regional]. A year earlier he hit one to win the super regional at Myrtle Beach. Entire team was incredible vs. UConn.

4. The win at Alabama to clinch the regular-season championship. If you win the SEC, you are damn good. It's an incredible league.

3. The second win vs. No. 1 Virginia. Incredible pitching. Unbelievable defense. Getting out of bases-loaded jams. And @AdamMatthews26 with the winner.

2. @ScottWingo8 play with Robert Beary's pick and Jake Williams' throw, @John_Taylor_14's double plays vs. Florida [in the first game of the championship series]. Some of the best plays in history of College World Series.

1. Watching the best center fielder in the country, @JackieBradleyJr, tracking the last fly ball. Knowing you are a few seconds away from a national championship!

Travis Haney's Twitter Timeline

@*TravHaney*
June 15–28

JUNE 15
Packing for trip like Omaha is easy: Throw everything you could possibly wear into bag, until it will not close. Remove two things. Go.

RT @BradyThomas36: OMAHA bound tomorrow!

Bradley Jr. UPDATE: More good news today. Hit off tee with no pain, took soft toss. Will take BP Thurs. On track to be on 27-man.

JUNE 16
RT @JoseMata17: Some flights are just a little more exciting than others. #OMAHA

Yes! RT @RooftopHeckler: @TravHaney a book on tape featuring Ray Tanner pronunciation of "series" would be awesome

RT @AdamMatthews26: How good it feels to be back in #Omaha #CarolinaBaseball

And we're back. Good to see ya, Omaha.

RT @cholbook2: The media is buzzing around our practice cause @JackieBradleyJr is getting ready to take bp

Bradley Jr. says no pain, thinks he's done enough to be on 27-man roster. We'll see what Tanner says.

Tanner says Bradley will be on CWS roster.

How much can Bradley play or help? I don't know. But I do know he couldn't do either if he weren't on roster. #cws

Tanner: "He looks good to go to me. The only thing that's missing is a lot of at-bats, a lot of repetition."

Columbia media (for most part) loves the Drover. Currently 9 of us dining at 2 tables. Plus some SC coaches behind us.

JUNE 17

RT @JackieBradleyJr. Romans 8:31 "If God is for us, who can be against us?" RT @michaudba: @JackieBradleyJr. do you have a favorite scripture verse?

Hey, @mtRoth29 is on a billboard. Big time.

I can't imagine any more Twitter-oriented teams than Gamecocks and Vandy. SC leading the way. You guys are fascinating. And weird.

Dining tonight at Lo Sole Mio, per the suggestion of one @aaronfitt. Missed this place a year ago.

LSU fans in Omaha, whether Tigers here or not, is most mystically wonderful tradition in sports. Seriously.

More @mtRoth29 head-inflating. RT @gogamecocks Michael Roth honored for having highest GPA (3.89) among CWS athletes.

Here he is trying to play humble. RT @mtRoth29: Officially the biggest nerd at the College World Series

New rule: Omaha is only place it's acceptable for Fogerty's Center Field to play.

June 18

Just drove past Rosenblatt. Honestly felt sadness emanating from the old girl.

We're underway at TDAP. Press box is incredible—and incredibly quiet. No open windows. Feel like I'm covering game at a library.

@Haney1075: "Maybe I shouldn't have eaten that piece of fat." #omaha #beef

June 19

In my projected lineup, I have Bradley starting in CF and hitting 7th. Can't risk more injury to Marzilli. Bradley in this big CF is plus.

I asked a couple of Gamecocks as they were walking who CF would be. Said only Tanner knows. We'll all know soon.

Jackie Bradley Jr. IS starting. Playing CF. Batting 2nd. (Later moved to No. 9 after Marzilli passed physical.)

Bradley starting didn't surprise me. Hitting second? Stunned me. With Marzilli showing he's fine, this lineup makes more sense.

Roth and Gamecocks finally out of first inning. But 4 runs score. Ouch. Tough start for Gamecocks.

All four runs are unearned. Incredible. Roth now given up 19 unearned runs. 14 earned runs.

Mooney ties game with infield single deep in 2B hole. New ballgame. What a weird inning. 4–4.

Scoreboard says—TAMU 4 runs, 2 hits, 1 error. South Carolina 4 runs, 3 hits, 1 error.

SC hadn't even scored in a CWS opener since 1982 until last year. Scored 3 runs in 2010 vs Okla. Plated 4 in 1st inning tonight.

That's awesome. Had a hunch he might do that. RT @2jonjacob BT initials shown clearly by cameras on Roth's cap… #baylerball

Get this: Roth has BT on his hat tonight. Bayler's mom is supposed to be in labor NOW with family's first girl. Seriously.

Rob Teal told me last night that Piper Teal was expected between 7–10 pm tonight. During game. Even though she was due Thurs.

Gamecocks relievers currently playing soccer with a beach ball. Sooo, in other words, no one's warming.

Through 5, TAMU—4 runs, 4 hits, 1 error. South Carolina—4 runs, 6 hits, 1 error.

Roth's high pitch count games this year: 124, 119, 115, 114, 114, 113, 111, 110. He has some experience in this department.

Roth at 120 pitches through 7. Give him bunch of credit for getting act together after first. Stretch time. STILL 4–4.

Roth is going back for 8th. Oook.

OK, now line final for Roth: 7.1 IP, 4 R (0 ER), 5 BB, 8 K. Taylor's 46th appearance of season.

As @Haney1075 points out, Roth gave up just two singles after first inning.

After that additional out, Roth's ERA still 0.97 (0.966).

Tie game in CWS vs Big 12 team that wears shade of red. I've seen this movie before.

RT @aaronfitt No question. RT @willkimmey: This has been the best game of the #CWS by far. Splendid baseball once we got out of first inning.

Of course, Bradley singles to LF. Beary standing on third base with 0 outs and top of order coming. That's incredible. Two months off, couldn't get bunt down and Bradley gets a crucial hit.

Marzilli walks on 5 pitches. How much do you love that Wingo is up with bases loaded in 9th?

Texas A&M brings in left fielder and Aggies will go with FIVE infielders. This is crazy.

Wingo has singled to right, bunted for a hit, doubled to right and been hit by pitch. On all four times up.

Wingo nearly hit grand slam. But, hey, it's a walk-off single. FOUR walk-off hits this year for Wingo.

Final: South Carolina 5, Texas A&M 4. Gamecocks win first CWS opener since 1977. Oh for last 7.

Wingo didn't have a legacy at South Carolina until tonight. Oh…wait…

Another chapter in the story was just written, friends. It would already be a pretty good book…

South Carolina has won 12 consecutive NCAA tourney games and seven straight in Omaha. Those numbers aren't bad.

Three of four teams in winner's bracket are from SEC—SEC East, actually. Virginia is the other.

Teal family update: Risha sent home from hospital for second consecutive night. Family watched game from hospital, home. Still waiting.

But Rob just told me how much it meant that @mtRoth29 had Bayler's initials on his cap tonight. A year later, BT's still making an impact.

RT @cholbrook@: It's a special group. They make me realize everyday what a lucky coach I am. Looking forward to a good night's rest.

I heard you, Big Man. Still hear you. RT @johnmwhittle: I've said it all year long—I just don't worry about this team.

#battlebattlebattle RT @mtRoth29: Had to #battle great win and going to enjoy day off tomorrow #DovesFlyTogether

This. Is. Not. Good. RT @JimCantore: Off to Omaha, NE early in the morning for a long week for #severe weather coverage.

Hey, @JimCantore, you never get maimed in weather disasters. I'm just going to hang with you tomorrow, OK? #cws

This is first night Omaha 2011 has felt like Omaha 2010. Guess it just took baseball to feel it.

JUNE 20

Good ? RT @fredontv: Time to start casting Gamecock Glory for the big screen? And who plays Ray Tanner? Gene Hackman is too old.

I can hear tornado sirens from my hotel room. Not good. But still playing ball at TDAP.

Ridiculous-looking line of storms just west of Omaha. Yikes. I'm wondering if stadium tunnel/basement is best place of me.

Omaha is scary right now. I tried to walk to stadium, but winds just went nuts. I had to turn back.

I don't get freaked out easily, but when I stepped out in that 40–50-mph wind, I turned around and hauled tail.

5 miles or so from TDAP. RT @TWCBreaking: Wind gust clocked at 69 mph at Omaha's Eppley Airfield.

Made a beeline for Drover after Oz-like weather passed. Because that's what we do. #scmedia

Omaha steak count: 3. RT @joshgandy: How many steaks have you had to #battle through thus far.

JUNE 21

RT @cholbrook2: Piper Teal was born less than hour ago. Pic of Rob lifting Natl Champ Trophy just days after BT's passing is still so clear.

Congrats to Rob and Risha Teal. What are the odds their first girl born on a Gamecocks gameday in Omaha? So happy for them.

RT @mtRoth29: Nobody needs to hate on @SteveWhiteVW. Dad quit on good terms. #gamecocknation needs to worry about cheering us on for tonight.

Bottom line: Roberts' 11-1, 1.58 ERA...stunning. BUT numbers are pretty modest in 6 starts vs ACC opponents 3-1 with 3-ish ERA.

So, Thomas does move down to 6. Tanner doesn't mess with Beary at 8 (don't blame him). But Bradley at 4? Wowzers. Va kid vs. UVa lineup?

Just got off phone little while ago with Rob Teal. Piper and mom resting well at hospital. She's in #baylerball T-shirt for tonight's game.

Piper Teal (8 lbs, 5 ozs) was born at 12:21 p.m. ET. Rob Teal: "I've never seen anything so beautiful." #chills

JBJ's first cleanup AB results—of course—in an RBI 2B to RCF. Walker scores from first. 1–0 SC. Wow.

Just teared up a little when Rob texted me what Piper's middle name is: Joelle. For Bayler Joel Teal. They'll always be connected.

Will Roberts' night is done before Virginia even got a hit. 11-1 on the year, but lasts just 3.1 innings tonight.

Cavs out of inning, but two more SC runs. 6–0 thru 3.5. Still long way to go.

ESPN says Charlie, teenage cancer survivor who befriended Tanner and SC years ago, is in Gamecocks' dugout.

Wingo hit by pitch for 60th time in his career. And his uniform is dirty. Sun also set in west today.

FINAL: Gamecocks 7, Virginia 1. SC has 5-2 record vs No. 1-ranked teams this season.

They just keep winning, folks. They show up every night and think they're supposed to win.

Virginia coach Brian O'Connor: "South Carolina, really, quite frankly beat us in every phase of the game."

Tanner: "We played probably one of our better games of the year tonight… in one of the biggest games of the year."

June 22
Can't imagine better compliment. Thank you. RT @dbmccaskill Your happiness is contagious. All the best to you. Many thanks for all you do.

SEC is one Gamecocks win away from three consecutive baseball national championships to go with five in football.

Just drove past Rosenblatt again. Still doesn't feel right. Feels like should be playing there.

JUNE 23
Based on what I've been told, if it's anyone other than Roth tomorrow, I'll be stunned. SC's just waiting as long as possible to announce.

JUNE 24
It's official now: Roth vs Hultzen tonight. Should be a good one.

I was told last night the only way Roth wouldn't pitch is if he suffered a freak injury, like overeating at Lo Sole Mio.

Bayler Joel Teal: Dec. 24, 2002–June 24, 2010. Remember him today. #battlelikebayler

A year ago on this date, Bayler died in the 8th inning of the 12-inning victory against Oklahoma in which SC was down to its last strike.

A year ago on this day, Michael Roth pitched a complete-game 3-hitter against Clemson with the initials BT on his cap.

Reporters in press box discussing who, hypothetically, would be SC's Sat starter. Five different answers.

Interesting from Tanner saying he wants 5–6 from Roth tonight. He just wanted 2–3 from him a year ago tonight.

Roth has outdueled three first-rounders this season—Gray, Meyer and Barnes. A fourth? His teammates help him?

RT @mtRoth29 #battlelikebayler

Hultzen strikes out side in 2nd, too. Another 0-2 breaking ball. Again, 12 pitches. SC isn't close.

If that's true about Hultzen being sick…I want whatever he's got.

Two relievers loosening in Virginia bullpen—and Hultzen has struck out every batter he's faced. This is incredible.

Seriously. This storyline fits with everything that's happened with SC the past two years here.

Crockett coming out of bullpen. Hultzen is done.

Danny Hultzen's epic night ends after 3: 3 IP, 1 H, 8 K. Wow. That's just stunning. How does that happen?

Misplayed ball in LCF. Should have been sac fly, but it's 2-run double for Thomas. Good contact. SC leads 2–1. Absurd how quickly this game has changed.

Anyone else think an ambulance would have had to come get Roth off the mound?

RT @SonnyGray2 I love watching Michael Roth pitch.

Roth's line: 7 IP, 4 H, 1 ER, 2 BB, 3 K, 1 HBP. 90 pitches, 56 for strikes. Another yeoman's outing.

Mooney cadillacked that groundball. Two errors in inning for SC, and the game is tied after ball through Mooney's legs.

Bayler has evidently requested extra innings. Both teams enter 10th with top of orders and closers on mound. New ballgame. Hit reset.

Anyone wants this game?

Kline at 100 pitches. 59 strikes. That's nuts. How is he standing?

Base hit, and let's go home. I wanna write.

No, not the 12th inning. Despite getting first two runners on, SC's 3-4-5 hitters can't even move the guys. Oy.

I don't think I've ever seen a reliever throw 100 pitches. Probably going to see two tonight.

SC botches the sac fielding, and Werman bunts for a hit. Gamecocks coming apart now. Bases loaded, 0 out for fading Price.

Price struck out Taylor, which is tough to do. Bases still loaded for Barr, who had 2 DPs other night but 0 all year before that.

Barr lines shot to Wingo, who flips to Mooney for DP. In-credible. Barr had not hit into DP in 235 ABs this season. Now 3 this week against SC.

Price didn't inherit that bases loaded, 0 out—like Coastal in 2010—but he got himself out of it. Unreal. 2–2, heading to bottom 13.

Kline's arm fell off. Winiarski is new pitcher for bottom 13. Kline K'd 7 and threw 107 pitches.

Seriously, this game a year after Bayler died?

An end to this #cws game, please! RT @JasonRomano Got the next 45 mins riding in the car. Anyone need prayer for anything??

Gamecocks win. Somehow. Wow. Two throwing errors on bunts send Matthews home with winner in the 13th.

Final: South Carolina 3, Virginia 2. Gamecocks and Gators will meet in an All-SEC final.

PS, Matt Price is a hero.

Gamecocks are 8-0 in NCAA tourney, just set NCAA record with 14 consecutive tourney W's.

Tanner: "I don't know where to begin."

RT @cholbrook2: Infreakingcredible! Comforting to know that Bayler was jumping up and down in heaven tonight, celebrating with his Gamecocks.

My favorite Roth quote on Price: "Sometimes I think he gets into jams on purpose."

Surprised you had the energy to tweet this. RT @MattPrice22: great game tonight we were able to come out on top good job boys

RT @aaronfitt: Man, I love baseball—just can't beat the drama we witnessed today. Days like this make me feel very lucky to do this job.

June 25
I was driving by when they literally took the Rosenblatt Stadium sign down. Toasting to it with a strawberry shake at Zesto.

RT @cholbrook2 3rd trip to the Drover is underway. It's a good thing when you can make more than two trips. Means you've been here a while.

June 26
SC's best hitter, Christian Walker, has some sort of wrist/hand injury. His status is "in question," Tanner says.

RT @cholbrook2 Adversity is our "normal"

Drover was like an SC team part—90 pct Gamecocks, at least. Thanks to Buddy and everyone else. What a treat, again.

June 27
Given what I've seen and heard, I'm expecting a 98–2 ratio of Gamecocks fans tonight. It's all garnet in Omaha.

SC confirms Christian Walker has hamate fracture in left hand/wrist. Specialists working with him now, to see if any way he can play.

I don't know that this changes a whole lot. Just matter of how much pain he can stand—without risking further injury.

Can't imagine how he could play with it. But those specialists will try to figure something out. Pct he plays has to be VERY slim.

RT @CWALK01313 Doing everything I can. It's in GOD's hands at this point.

RT @CWALK01313 Big time players make big time plays in big time situations. #gamecockbaseball

Neff and Roth taking grounders at first base.

Here's SC lineup (for now): Wingo 2B, Mooney SC, Bradley CF, Thomas DH, Morales 3B, Williams LF, Marzilli RF, Beary C, Roth 1B. Obviously, this could change—right up until gametime.

Walker's first BP swing is a home run into bullpen. Seriously. Just cleared fence. Had some help with wind. But…that really happened.

Question is, How much pain is Walker in? He didn't seem to like that last swing, a pop-up into the cage net.

In his fourth round of BP, Walker hit two HRs—one in bullpen and one about 400-ft to LCF gap. Walker's last swings—two more homers. He's got to be in there, right?

What a last-minute emotional lift that has to be for a team, to watch your best hitter #battle to get in lineup. #cws

New lineup: Wingo 2B, Bradley CF, WALKER 1B, Thomas DH, Morales 3B, Williams LF, Mooney SS, Beary C, Marzilli RF.

All Christian Walker does in his first AB is double down the RF line. First pitch. Crazy stuff.

Gators smallball in first run. Walk, FC, WP, sac fly scores Thompson. 1–0 UF. Koumas had chance to nail lead runner earlier.

Randall is #dealing. Two K's in 5th. Retired 12 of past 13. 1–0 UF thru 4.5.

I'm plenty impressed with Koumas so far. Gutsy. Run on two hits, and run scored because of walk, groundout, wild pitch, sac fly.

Make it 15 of 16 retired for Randall. He's making this look easy. 1–0 UF thru 5.5. #cws

Randall with a six-pitch 7th. Under 70 pitches through 7. This is what he does. Stretch time. SC needs offense. 1–0 UF.

Randall has retired 18 of 19, 10 in row. Mooney-Beary-PH will try to change fortunes in 8th.

Mooney makes Randall work to start 8th. Walks on five pitches. Beary gets bunt down, moves Mooney to 2B with 1 down.

Marzilli flies to CF. Mooney took BIG risk getting to third, but wide throw saved him. Tying run 90 feet away for Wingo, who's been awful tonight.

Wingo pokes shot up middle, past Randall and into CF. Unreal. Tie game. 1–1. Randall done. Game-changer.

Gamecocks in big trouble now in bottom 9 after Johnson, who couldn't get bunt down, singles to right. Zunino (winning run) on third. This obviously is where no Price is a killer.

Taylor will intentionally walk Adams to bring up Tyler Thompson. Bases loaded and none out. Going to take more magic from SC pen.

Sharp grounder to Wingo, who fires home to Beary to get lead runner. Now 1 down. Saves the game. Far from out of danger, though. What a play by Wingo to spin and fire home. Good pick by Beary, too, playing his best first base.

Holy s---. Wingo-Beary-Walker. 4-2-3 double play ends 9th. My goodness.

OK, that one I cannot believe. Can't believe it. Two hard-hit balls—right to Wingo. Just when you thought this was over…

I mean, all it took was a fly ball. Anything. And now they'll get more hacks vs Maddox. Truly incredible. #battle #cws

RT @aaronfitt: #SouthCarolina should be required to be in #CWS every year. Nobody gives us better drama, game after game. This one is a real dandy.

I'm sure Taylor would prefer a much less dramatic 10th inning. 9-1-2 due for UF.

Taylor gets fly ball for 2nd out, now walking LHH Tucker—to get to SEC POY Zunino. Ballsy, but going matchups.

What the hell. Williams, with a modest arm, perfect throw to nail Dent out at plate after Zunino single to left. STILL 1–1. This is insane.

As soon as Zunino put that one in LF, I said, out loud "it's over." But Williams came up with it and put the ball on the money to Beary.

This is just silly. Three of four games SC has played here have been some of the best I've seen in my life. They refuse to lose. Really.

No offense to Williams. But that was a one-in-20-tries throw. Good time for it, Jake.

That's three Gators thrown out at plate in past two innings. Just one of them touches before ball, and this is over.

Walker with his second hit of night. He steals second. Throw is airmailed. Then another bad throw to third. Walker SCORES from first. E2. E8. SC LEADS 2–1.

This beats the hell out of anything I've ever seen in any sporting venue.

Tanner sent a runner with a broken hand. And he went into second head-first. And then feet-first to third. Crazy stuff.

RT @ESPN_CWSKyle This is a movie. Christian Walker steals 2nd, two throwing errors score Walker. Gamecocks lead 2–1, Price warming in the pen.

72 hours after he threw 95 pitches, Matt Price being summoned for three outs. I'm sure he'd like fewer than 95 tonight.

How's everyone's nerves at home? Long gone, I'm sure.

Price is 94–96 right now. He's been 90–92 all year. #adrenaline

Mooney to Walker. It's over. A-MAZ-ING. One win from another national title. How many times did UF win that game? But SC wins 2–1.

Best game I've ever seen. And I've seen lots of good ones from this SC team. Hollywood would not have to doctor this script one bit.

Walker needs surgery, Tanner says, but doctors have told him he is not risking further injury. Just a matter of pain. Walker has nuts.

RT @cholbrook2: An incredible win against an incredible team. Gotta keep playin.

RT @CWALK01313: Unbelievable. This team is crazy. #gamecockbaseball

June 28

RT @sketchbookb Really hope @TravHaney gets to write "Gamecock Encore" #OneMoreWin #gogamecocks

How about this: I'll at least admit I'd like to see one more win. I know what it would mean. RT @grahamcouch are you a gamecock fan yet?

Roth. I'm 101 percent sure. RT @IdrinkJAGER who's on the mound tonight? NO way it's Roth…is it?

Just stepped into a PERFECT Omaha morning. I don't take that for granted. Headed to play catch. Because that's what we do.

Text I just received from friend: "Garcia is sitting next to us at the Drover." #winning

RT @DaleMurphy3 Pulling for the #gamecocks in #cws! Repeat for the "real" USC!

A mom asked me to sign a book for her daughter with something encouraging. I told her to "channel her inner Wingo."

I think a lot of us just assumed Walker would be fine today, just because he played Monday. Should have considered swelling.

Walker IS in the lineup. Giving it a go. What else did you expect? #battle

Wingo has been hit five times in this CWS, tying a record. That's a record you'd expect Wingo to hold.

Whitson FINALLY out of inning. Took 35 pitches. Three SC runs in, two of them unearned. 3–0 SC thru 3.

Zunino's homer is only third Roth has given up all year in 140.1 IP.

Gamecocks finally have a CWS. As you'd expect, it's Peter Mooney. Wait, Peter Mooney? 4–1 SC. Mooney's last homer, we're told, was May 10—vs the Blue Hose of Presbyterian.

RT @JennBrownESPN He wrote BT for Bayler Teal. The boy who passed last yr from cancer. RT @westonbmay: Charlie wrote something in the dirt. What was it?

Roth guts through 7th, works around leadoff walk. He really held it together to get three more. 4–1 SC at stretch.

Roth over 120 pitches again. Done it all year. But this is a lot of guts, on 3 days' rest. Meyers going to get Roth now. 127 pitches, according to ESPN. Roth's career CWS numbers—1.17 ERA in 38 1/3 IP. Second-lowest ERA among pitchers with 30+ IP.

Price—95 pitches Friday, 16 pitches Monday. What's he got left for final 4 outs? Adrenaline going full blast, I'm sure.

Gamecocks: Three outs from a repeat. #cws

Johnson to Bradley. Two outs to title.

Grounder to Walker. Takes it himself. ONE out to title. #cws

The Gamecocks are again glorious in Omaha. National champions. Again.

It's over. FINAL: South Carolina 5, Florida 2. Wins series 2-0. Gamecocks finish 55-14.

I haven't even had a conversation with publisher, but, yeah, expect @ gamecockglory sequel.

I can't believe that just happened again. Wasn't it just February?

Wrap your mind around this—Scott Wingo. Most Outstanding Player of College World Series. That happened.

Scott Wingo just said, "We don't give you 1 yard" in the postgame—of a baseball game. That's classic. #wingo

Roth, to me, as he left presser: "Good luck with that book." #sequel

The 2011 University of South Carolina baseball team.

About the Author

Travis Haney has covered University of Oklahoma sports for the *Oklahoman* in Oklahoma City, Oklahoma, since August 2011. He previously followed University of South Carolina sports for the *Post and Courier* for four and a half years. While in that position, he chronicled the Gamecocks' two NCAA baseball championships, writing *Gamecock Glory* in 2011 about the team's first national title. Haney also spent more than two seasons covering the Atlanta Braves for Morris News Service. Haney, thirty, has won numerous writing awards and had a 2004 feature story published in the *Best American Sports Writing* series. He lives in Norman, Oklahoma.